The Art and Design Teacher's Handbook

Also available from Continuum

Art Education 11-18 2nd Edition, Richard Hickman
Sounds Like a Good Idea, Mike Kinnaird

The Art and Design Teacher's Handbook

Susie Hodge

A companion website to accompany this book is available online at:
   http://education.hodge3.continuumbooks.com
   Please visit the link and register with us to receive your password and to access these downloadable resources.
   If you experience any problems accessing the resources, please contact Continuum at: info@continuumbooks.com

continuum

Continuum Internatinoal Publishing Group

The Tower Building   80 Maiden Lane
11 York Road   Suite 704
SE1 7NX   New York, NY 10038

www.continuumbooks.com

British Library Cataloguing-in-Publication Data
A catalogue record for this book is available from the British Library.

ISBN: 9781847061508 (paperback)

Library of Congress Cataloging-in-Publication Data
Hodge, Susie, 1960–
     Art and design teacher's handbook / Susie Hodge.
       p. cm.
     ISBN 978-1-84706-150-8 (pbk.)
     1. Art–Study and teaching (Secondary) 2. Design–Study and teaching (Secondary)   I. Title.
   N363.H63 2010
   707.1′2–dc22

                                      2009037862

Typeset by BookEns, Royston, Herts.
Printed and bound in Great Britain

Contents

Introduction: A positive start

Art education is unlike any other subject. While this could be said of any subject taught in schools today, art and design is particularly diverse. Most art teachers are practising artists – they have either worked in some kind of art and design profession before training as teachers or they continue to work as artists or designers while teaching. This is one of the many unique aspects of art teaching – and a particularly positive one. Art practitioners are fully equipped to impart informed knowledge about their skills and current practices. They frequently enter teaching to share their passion for art and to inspire others to feel the same enthusiasm for the subject. Another unusual aspect of the subject in schools is that the content is not laid down specifically, yet it relies on the coverage of a broad range of aims and objectives in order to justify its purpose and to guide pupils through an essential range of skills and knowledge.

Art and design teaches young people visual literacy, critical and creative thinking and, of course, the essential skills, techniques and theories connected with the subject. It helps students to develop abilities in reflection, intuition and articulacy. It enhances emotional intelligence and cultural and aesthetic awareness. It encourages both creative and critical thinking and although most students will not become artists, many will become consumers of art, craft and design.

Finally, the creative industries are vast and expanding. Creative people are desperately needed in the workforce – more than ever before. Unfortunately, for some though, art retains a reputation as a 'soft' subject – perhaps because unlike many others, there are no right or wrong answers. Anyone who has taught art and design, however, knows that it can be one of the most challenging yet rewarding subjects in the school curriculum. Art teachers continually have to keep lessons relevant and

1

engaging while embracing new technologies and media. Lessons have to incorporate these new developments along with new directions given by curriculum authorities, exam boards and senior management teams.

Most schools rightly and proudly display the products of their art departments on corridor walls and in display cabinets. This is often the first visual sign to visitors of what is going on in an establishment and of how it perceives itself; the showcase of the entire school. Yet although the quality of art produced is a good indication of the effectiveness of a department, it is not always enough to prove the success of art and design within the school. Further evidence is needed and although most art teachers are dedicated, passionate and multi-faceted, even the most enthusiastic can baulk at some of the new initiatives, assessment and syllabus changes that are frequently introduced. Newly qualified art teachers can be forgiven for wondering what they have let themselves in for: combining a detailed and in depth knowledge of theory with versatile and comprehensive practical skills. Somewhere in there, job satisfaction and sanity have to be preserved, without any sacrifices – and it can be done!

This handbook is intended to provide practical support for secondary school art and design teachers across Key Stages (KS) 3, 4 and 5. You can know your subject well and be able to balance a range of objectives, long and short term planning and assessment criteria, but sometimes you can feel a bit isolated and overwhelmed. It is all too easy to lose your enthusiasm and intentions in an effort to keep up with the workload, so this book is to try to help restore or maintain these. When things become too frantic, stop for a moment and remember who inspired you the most at school – the dull and dreary teacher who taught you methodically but monotonously, or the interested teacher with a passion for the subject? Hold that thought! Although you need to be organized and efficient, this is not the most effective way of teaching. Your reasons for teaching in the first place – your zeal for and interest in art – should remain at the forefront of your teaching, whatever your responsibilities or new directives. This book is here to give you new ideas and hopefully to help level out your workload. It examines different ways in which teachers can respond to and take advantage of the many positive aspects of the subject, while still addressing the required attainment targets. It includes suggestions to help the development of skills and imagination through a variety of different content areas and teaching situations. Each chapter aims to help you help your pupils develop insight, fluency, analytical and critical abilities, historical, cultural and aesthetic understanding, creativity and practicality. It will help you to develop flexible approaches and ideas to enhance your teaching. Focusing on many of the challenging issues of secondary school art education, including why and how we teach art to older children and teenagers, the book gives suggestions for planning and delivering lessons, as well as raising attainment at all stages – from Year 7 to Year 13.

Across the globe, art lessons in secondary schools give pupils opportunities to explore visual, tactile and other sensory experiences in order to communicate ideas and meanings. They are encouraged to work with a variety of media, investigating and developing their creativity, practical skills, manual dexterity, aesthetic awareness and manipulation of materials. By reflecting on their own and others' work, evaluating quality and meaning, they learn to appreciate images and artefacts across times and cultures and to understand the contexts in which they were made. Young people who have valuable experiences in school art studies are disposed to become discriminating arts consumers and contributors in later life. This book guides you through a great deal of approaches and ideas to help you plan, create and organize your teaching and hopefully, reduce or balance your workload, while boosting your confidence and ideas.

Art education during the early teen years gives pupils ways of identifying themselves and the wider world that is not taught in other subjects. A good education can also enhance thinking, personal development, confidence and learning in other subjects. In the *Education Reform Act* of 1988, art became one of the ten compulsory subjects of the English National Curriculum at KS3. In many other countries too, art is an essential part of the curriculum for students during their adolescent years. Most pupils enjoy working in a practical and creative environment, with opportunities to express themselves in new and original ways, exploring their identities and challenging assumptions. Many art lessons also provide opportunities for investigating personal concerns and emotions and developing structures for values and beliefs. By collaborating with others, working in groups and taking part in discussions, art students also develop skills in communication, critical thinking and creative problem solving. Health and safety is part of the process and the understanding of safe practices in the working environment is integral to students' collection of skills learned in the art department.

This book considers how to create, modify and apply worthwhile resources and teaching ideas, as well providing advice for planning, organization and how to reduce any drudgery or tedium. At the end of the book, you will hopefully have several methods to put in place to aid your teaching and enrich your students' learning, as well as reinforcing your own self-confidence and sense of achievement and pleasure in teaching.

The aims and purposes of art at this age

The impact of a great art teacher can resonate throughout students' lives, influencing their hobbies, lifestyles, attitudes and tastes for years after actual teaching ceases. Yet while schools continue to measure success only through exam achievement, this is rarely taken into account. Establishing and maintaining the equilibrium between encouraging an understanding and appreciation of art, craft and design and coaching to achieve high grades might often seem like an insurmountable paradox – but it needn't be!

The right balance

Always at the forefront of education in any subject is the issue of how to raise attainment, so it is important to consider how you are developing and advancing students' learning skills. In art, it has been ascertained that from the ages of 11 to 14, about 60 per cent of pupils make reasonable progress, while approximately 20–30 per cent are bored and either behave badly or simply stop listening, leaving the remaining 10–20 per cent simply treading water. In addition, there are disparities between the achievements of boys and girls. There will always be such problems in a compulsory subject, but there are ways to confront and deal with them.

It is crucial to get the right balance in your art lessons. However interesting your lessons might be to you, unless you engage and sustain individuals' interests, you will not raise attainment. Select subjects that they can connect with and will find absorbing. If this works for one class but not for another, try adapting your approach, the materials they use, the scale they work to or even the artists or designers you suggest to inspire them. Art lessons must include variety, pace and challenge. Students will respond to these features best if they feel secure and comfortable. They should enjoy their lessons, but also need to be motivated to work and learn. If you focus less on what you want the class to learn and more on how this learning will take place, you keep a manageable sense of pace and create the right balance of enjoyment and learning. This will in turn lead to greater attainment at the end of Key Stages (KS) 3, 4 and 5.

The curriculum

KS3 should be a continuation of pupils' creative and expressive development from primary school, including an exploration of technical skills and practical experience. Students are expected to make progress in various skills and need to show that they can:

- Explore and develop ideas by initiating research critically and evaluating ideas, research, document and present ideas in ways that are visually appropriate.
- Investigate and create, by exploiting the characteristics of materials and processes, sustaining their investigations to fully realize their intentions.
- Evaluate and develop their work by identifying the reasons for different interpretations of ideas and meanings, clearly communicating views and insights.

From the age of 14, art and design becomes elective, leading to external exams at 16 plus, which are usually GCSEs at 16, or Year 11, AS at 17 or Year 12, and A2 at 18 or Year 13. All exam boards have common criteria and credence is given to the quality of investigation and research that prompts the making of good quality images and artefacts. Art and design is one of the most popular options at GCSE, with an average of 40 per cent of all school children choosing to take it. At this level, many art teachers achieve high levels of motivation and response from students of greatly differing abilities, which says a great deal for the value of art education in schools. GCSE and A level specifications have comparable assessment objectives in knowledge, understanding and skills. Good planning of lessons and resources are imperative here – only by knowing what and how

Ways in which children should progress in art and design at Key Stage 3

	Year 7	Year 8	Year 9
Exploring and developing ideas	Students ask and answer relevant questions. They are able to choose their own viewpoints and select and develop from their ideas and experiences. They collect, record, explore ideas and gather information in their sketchbooks to use as a basis for developing work.	Students ask and answer questions about source materials. They select viewpoints and develop ideas and experiences as a response. They are able to record, collect and collate information and begin to explore and experiment with ideas and information in their sketchbooks.	Students are able to discuss and query critically. They can select and analyze ideas and experiences for different purposes. They are able to record and research, gathering information in their sketchbooks.
Investigating and making art, craft and design	Students have developed and improved their control of various tools, techniques and materials. They can experiment with and combine visual and tactile qualities of materials and processes. They have used drawing in different ways as required: planning, observing, recording and designing.	Students can control and develop different tools and techniques for specific purposes. By experimenting with materials, they develop knowledge of properties and processes that they apply to suit their requirements. They interpret ideas and use different media to achieve several effects.	Students can select, combine and manipulate materials and images. They have extended their knowledge and experience of a range of materials and processes, refining their control of tools and techniques. They can select from and interpret ideas and realize their intentions in a range of media.
Evaluating and developing work	Students compare ideas and approaches to their own and others' work. They can explain their views using a specialist vocabulary. They adapt their work where appropriate and work out how to further develop pieces.	Students can compare and contrast ideas and approaches to their own and others' work. They augment their practical work with specialist terminology and they adapt and change their work appropriately.	Students can reflect on and evaluate their own and others' work and can express informed opinions. They modify and refine their work appropriately and plan and develop this, further taking into account their own and others' observations.

| Knowledge and understanding | Students know and understand how visual elements can be combined and organized for a variety of purposes; how ideas and observations are represented in works of art, craft and design; how materials and processes are used; and the role and purposes of artists, craftspeople and designers working in different times and cultures. | Students can make informed observations about works of art, craft and design. They know and understand how visual and tactile elements can be combined and altered to represent different meanings and purposes; how ideas and beliefs are represented in works of art, craft and design; and how beliefs and values change or continue over time across different cultures. | Students can manipulate materials, processes, visual and tactile qualities. They are aware of codes and conventions and how artists, craftspeople and designers have represented ideas and beliefs in their work. Continuity and change have been explored in the purposes and audiences of artists, craftspeople and designers across different times and cultures. |

they will be learning and preparing for unexpected eventualities will you be able to encourage high levels of motivation and application. If you allow for flexibility, your students will develop with greater alacrity and in broader terms than if you adhere rigidly to your set plans. This is not actually contradictory – the more well-organized and prepared you are, the easier it is to allow students to branch off and develop in different ways. The previous chart shows ways in which children should progress in art and design at KS3.

The following chart shows some descriptions and features of various grades at different stages in students' secondary education.

Both charts are also online in case you would like to display them on the board or print them off and give them out to your students.

Scope and limitations

Acknowledgment that creativity can increase confidence is becoming more prevalent and some of the changes in art education have arisen from this, including ways in which the subject is managed within the curriculum and in the wider scope of the school. There are always fashions and fads in educational practices and it's up to those at the interactive whiteboard face to keep these things rational and effective. At present, some of the most debated topics in teaching are: assessment for learning (AfL), gifted and talented (G&T) and differentiation for pupils with special educational needs (SEN). AfL is important because it is all about helping students to understand how and why they are being assessed. From the start, familiarize students with the assessment criteria in language they understand. Refer to it often. You will soon be aware of any G&T students in your subject as these are usually chosen by subject teachers for outstanding work or effort. Before teaching any new class, you should have been made aware of students with any SEN and possibly have been given strategies for helping them. Whatever extras you have to deal with, always keep lesson objectives firmly in your mind. Another issue that might cause concern when you first start teaching is when certain students opt to take art at GCSE, believing it to be an 'easy option'. They soon learn, of course that it is a complex subject that requires time and effort,

Some descriptions and features of various grades at different stages in students' secondary education

Year 9	Year 11	Year 13
Characteristics of a Level 7: Students explore ideas and assess a range of information, which they select, organize and present in various ways for different purposes. They have an informed understanding of materials and processes, which they use in their work. They work quite independently, developing ideas and realizing their intentions. They can analyze and discuss the contexts of their own and others' work and can explain how their experiences and values affect their work and views. They can analyze codes and conventions used by artists, craftspeople and designers.	**Characteristics of a Grade A GCSE:** Students explore, interpret and express their ideas and feelings fluently, sensitively and imaginatively. They use a wide range of source material effectively and can analyze ideas to develop their investigations. They make coherent use of the key elements, developing their work using informed judgements. They assess artefacts and images critically, recognize different interpretations of value and meaning, understand that conventions change with time and place and are able to articulate opinions and preferences using a specialist vocabulary.	**Characteristics of a Grade A A2 level:** Student's work is personal, sustained and inventive. It shows independence of thought, original ideas and a high level of visual enquiry. The work is distinctive and unique, showing a secure grasp of media, process and techniques. There is evidence of lively experimentation and exploration. Depth and breadth of knowledge and a firm sensitivity for aesthetic qualities are exploited. Clarity of expression, refined sensitivity, critical judgement and awareness is evident. Imaginative and fluent responses and intentions are realized in a coherent and highly competent manner.
Characteristics of a Level 5: Students explore ideas and can select visual and other information. They manipulate materials and processes to communicate ideas and meanings and they are able to produce artwork that matches their intentions. They can consider and comment on ideas, methods	**Characteristics of a Grade C GCSE:** Students record and analyze observations and express ideas and feelings, communicating meaning in visual form. They select and organize relevant information, experimenting with materials, processes and ideas, working independently. They understand	**Characteristics of a B Grade A level:** Students show enthusiasm and some independent thought. Work displays distinctive qualities, but development of ideas is restricted. Techniques, processes and media are used confidently but are unrefined. There is evidence of experimentation, exploration and selection that communicate intentions.

many materials, tools and techniques and they can select and interpret the key elements, adapting their work to realize their intentions. They can assess images and artefacts critically; identifying characteristics of works from a range of styles, cultures and periods. They endorse their views using specialist vocabulary.

Work is organized to show ideas and information and some attempts at evaluating have been made. Creative responses realize personal intentions and connections are made with their work. Views are validated with specialist terminology.

and approaches used by themselves and others and relate these to particular contexts. They adapt and refine their work to reflect their own views of its purpose and meaning.

Characteristics of a Level 3:
Students explore ideas and can collect visual and other information for their work. They investigate the qualities of materials and processes used, are able to communicate their ideas and meanings and can produce final pieces for different purposes. They can comment on similarities and differences between their own and others' work and can adapt and improve their own.

Characteristics of a Grade E/F GCSE:
Students select and record observations and present ideas. They collect visual information and evidence to support their ideas and they experiment with source material, showing development of ideas. They experiment with materials, tools and techniques with some control and expression. They can identify some methods used to create some artefacts and images, relating these to the times and cultures in which they were created. Students can discuss the characteristics of artworks and show some ability to support their opinions using a restricted specialist vocabulary.

Characteristics of a C Grade A2 level:
Students show evidence of interest and effort together with some creativity in the search and exploration for new ideas. There will be an inconsistent reliance on secondary sources and some evidence of understanding of the use of elementary techniques and processes. Materials are used with some care and thought. Aesthetic understanding and skills are limited. Some work describes the views and ideas of others using a restricted specialist vocabulary.

but motivating such pupils often remains a problem. Short bursts of different activities, plenty of interaction and a variety of ways of presenting information are some of the ways in which art teachers can motivate their students.

Art and design programmes of study are purposefully flexible to allow art departments the freedom to tailor learning to benefit different classes and even individual students' needs. There are many ways of teaching the subject and an infinite variety of subjects, themes and topics that can be included. This flexibility should also allow for more differentiation and for teachers to teach topics that they feel particularly confident in. For instance, you may have a student who is in Year 9 demonstrating many of the skills required in Years 10 and 11, so you can incorporate some more demanding goals in your lessons for that particular pupil. Sometimes however, the breadth of possibilities and scope can add to the problems in getting everything covered – colleagues may have conflicting preferences or ideas. Extremely flexible departments can end up with pupils reaching Year 10 never having used clay or produced a lino-print, for instance, while others might have done so much 3D work that students' painting skills are minimal. On the other hand, a rigid department, whereby all the teachers must follow set schemes of work, can ignore or stifle an individual teacher's unique skills and in this way shortchange itself as students will miss out on potential benefits.

Art teachers don't need to be told how valuable their subject is in the curriculum. Art lessons are one of the few occasions in a pupil's week where he or she is not collecting and storing secondhand information, but is frequently creating something new and original. Whether pupils have special skills and aptitudes towards art, or they have SEN, art teachers are in the position to make every lesson worthwhile, meaningful and enlightening, so that not only are the subject's results raised, but in consequence students' experience of secondary education is enhanced overall.

The significance of making

One of the exclusive aspects of art education is the making of original artworks and artefacts. Making things can significantly improve confidence and self-perception. At whatever level this reaches, creativity means that students make choices reflecting personal perceptions, their environments and experiences. All art education nurtures creativity, intuition, reasoning, imagination and dexterity, but how much students get out of it depends on their attitudes and willingness to learn and how much you can motivate them. By enabling your students to actively explore their visual perceptions and presumptions, their confidence and awareness of their cultural and visual surroundings will increase. This also helps to extend their ability to engage with society on many levels. By giving your pupils the relevant tools, even those with low abilities or expectations should be able to make valid decisions in situations where there are no standard answers. Even deciding that a piece of creative work has not turned out as intended can be empowering for a child and this can lead to perceptiveness and sensitivity.

Changes

The transition from primary to secondary school can be daunting for a child of 11, but art lessons can be a particularly positive part of the adaptation process. The emotional, physical and intellectual changes that occur in the first three years at secondary school can be enormous and particular art projects can help to acclimatize children to these changes. The merits of exploring issues through their own experiences can be enormously helpful in the ways in which they adjust to all those changes and learn about the circles they inhabit and the world around them. In Year 7, children face new social roles as well as the contrast between a smaller primary school and a much larger secondary school. If at this stage you include a variety of group-based activities and discussions, pupils will learn to analyze, investigate and make comparisons far more quickly than they might have done if working entirely in isolation.

The importance of making the art learning environment enjoyable as pupils progress through the years cannot be overemphasized. Maintaining their interest inspires them to participate more and so develop greater awareness of their own and others' needs, enabling them to respond with confidence to their individual and personal view of themselves and their world. Creative aptitudes – such as creativity, imagination and spatial awareness – are inherent and are acquired while developing the capacity to research, analyze and draw. By helping students to develop in this way – to put aside preconceived attitudes; to gain skills and knowledge; and to modify or completely change their original ideas to create finished concepts – you will be enabling young people to develop holistically.

◆ *Taking risks*

After about the age of ten, many children become self-conscious about their drawing skills and more susceptible to criticism and peer pressure. Whereas earlier in their education you could ask a class to draw, say, a fire engine, everyone would do so without hesitation, once they reach secondary school most children become insecure about their drawing abilities and are concerned about what others may think of them. So from this age, helping children to want to gain greater drawing skills is an operation that should be handled with sensitivity.

Apart from dealing with bad behaviour, clumsy or critical comments at this time can crush a child's confidence, restricting development. Similarly, appraisal and assessment needs to be tactful, encouraging and constructive. From the start, let your pupils know that it is important to take risks. This could be in their ideas or uses of materials. Even if things go wrong, risk taking gives pupils the tools they need to make and correct their own mistakes and evaluate their own work, so becoming independent learners. Risk taking might not just come from the pupils. You may want to try out a fresh teaching idea. If it doesn't work, let pupils know what you tried and see whether they can suggest ways in which you might remedy it. These are ways you will build up a rapport with each class and individual pupils.

From the start, where possible offer opportunities to work with a wide variety of materials under different conditions. By knowing when to step back and when to step in, you will enable your students to cope with frustration and failure, so that they develop the courage to try new and unusual ideas. It's not always easy with just one lesson a week, so you might want to organize lunchtime or after school clubs, where your students can practise and experiment with materials and techniques. Apart from the specific requirements of a project, at all times emphasize that whatever students produce, it must be *relevant*; they must show *control* of the materials they are using; they must take *ownership* of whatever they are doing; they should aim to be *innovative*. It is vital to get the right balance between experiences that allow for objective and expressive responses.

Facing facts

Many art teachers face considerable challenges. Less than 25 per cent of secondary schools require all pupils at KS4 to study at least one arts subject and only 13 per cent allow every pupil to take art and design if they wish to do so. Class sizes for art and design are generally higher than the average for all subjects taken together, so ensuring that you give each pupil in exam classes enough of your time can be difficult. On the other hand, art remains one of the most popular subjects at KS4, which means you have a positive start! With these issues in mind, it is worth doing a quick review of the available skills in your department, so you can utilize everyone's abilities in the best possible ways. There is a questionnaire that you might like to fill in and reflect on online.

Teaching creative thinking

From their first art lessons at secondary school, children can be encouraged to think creatively. As already discussed, thinking skills are a natural part of art lessons. Studies show that highly creative people have particularly fluent and flexible minds, which allows them to think of unusual, unique and original ideas quickly. But first your pupils need to acquire plenty of background knowledge, as creative thinkers need to know a lot about their subject. Then they can manipulate facts and combine them in new ways.

Foster creative thinking by encouraging your pupils to research thoroughly and then make lists and sketches – even stick men or the briefest symbols are helpful in the formation of thoughts. While this may be your regular way of working for students over 14, by introducing the concept earlier on you will establish creative thinking skills. Drawing, thumbnail sketches, making lists and mind maps are all effective ways of generating ideas or solving problems. Students should be as expansive as they can when working on these as this can help build unconventional and unexpected ideas. Some students find making long lists easy, while others struggle, so you might find it helpful to put them with partners or in small groups to contribute to and work up ideas. Remind everyone to concentrate on the process of developing ideas rather than the final outcome; i.e. process over product. A great deal of our analyzing and creating occurs at a subconscious level and often fresh ideas rise to the conscious mind when we are not expecting it, which is why these methods work.

Encourage everyone to try one or more of the three methods frequently. The more they practise, the more ideas they will generate. When you give them a brief for any project, they shouldn't grasp the first idea they have, but keep thinking and listing or drawing until a less obvious solution or idea forms. They do not have to be systematic, but should draw or list things that interest them, almost at random as long as it is relevant in some way to the topic or creative problem you have posed for them. There are no right or wrong answers or ideas, so they shouldn't worry about outcomes.

Drawing to aid thinking skills

Drawing is an extremely useful creative thinking tool. It assists in the development of many kinds of creative ideas and in problem solving. It is not the straight imitation of secondary sources that so many admire. (How many parents come to you at parents' evening and tell you 'Jo/e is really artistic. S/he can copy anything'?) Drawing is a skill that can be artistic and creative, but not always. Observational drawing can be learned by almost anybody at nearly any age. Researchers have found that observational drawing comes from the right side of the brain where intuitive and creative thinking occurs, which seems to indicate that observational drawing practice develops the intuitive, visualizing part of the brain. People who work in the creative industries use the drawing process to work out concepts and create ideas. Similarly, when they practise both expressive and observational drawing, students naturally develop their own creative thinking skills. So it is extremely important to teach observational drawing skills, but try not to become too prescriptive. Encourage your pupils to visualize and imagine as well. Their experiences may be limited, but dreams and the imagination should be nurtured and cultivated in order to

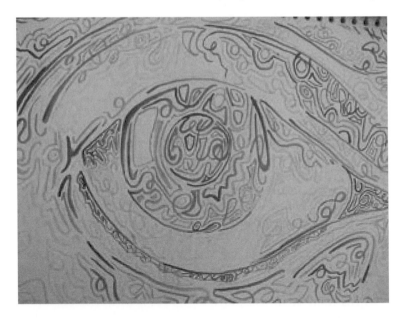

Exploring line and pattern as part of a creative journey, from a Year 12 work journal, Westcliff High School for Girls, Westcliff-on-Sea, Essex

Expressive drawing from direct observation, with relevant annotations to explain the thought process. Year 12 work journal, Westcliff High School for Girls, Westcliff-on-Sea, Essex

support creative thinking. Some quick exercises to encourage creative thinking in KS3 children are available online.

Using contemporary art

Recent research indicates that only a minority of schools use contemporary visual art in their learning programmes, despite evidence that these are valuable methods for learning and meeting many objectives in the art room as well as helping students to consider contemporary society and other issues. A key component of art and design lessons is the opportunity for pupils to develop a breadth of study and critical understanding through investigating different kinds of work and understanding art in a broad context. Contemporary art frequently confronts socio-cultural questions that may be relevant to many young people's understanding of their identity and of the world we live in.

Apart from the broad range of materials used, contemporary artists are often concerned with a wide range of concepts, rather than just aesthetics. This gives teachers great opportunities for

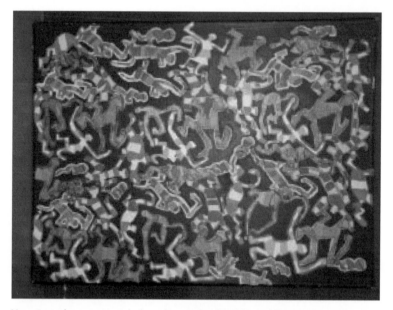

Year 9 students responded to the work of Keith Haring in paint and string prints. Year 9 students, Loreto College, St Alban's, Hertfordshire

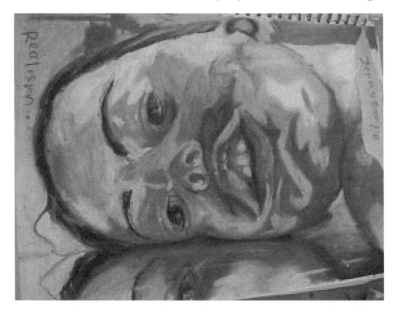

CAPTION 2: Response to Jenny Saville, Year 13 painting, Westcliff High School for Girls, Westcliff-on-Sea, Essex

helping pupils to place themselves at the centre of their own learning by drawing on their own personal experiences. Many modern artists are concerned with nature, identity, society, technology and conventions – concepts that lend themselves to practical activities and responses in the art rooms. Some useful (in terms of inspiring wide ranging responses) contemporary artists include Andy Goldsworthy, Meret Oppenheim, Anya Gallacio, Cornelia Parker, Bill Viola, Yinka Shonibare, Gillian Wearing, Cindy Sherman and Mariko Mori. Many of these artists celebrate cultural variety and difference, which are essential areas of understanding for future adults.

Using contemporary art in art lessons helps to broaden students' understanding of what constitutes art and art practice. It helps to invigorate their interest and engagement and could change the dynamics of a class (for instance, formerly quiet pupils often have more to contribute when they see everyday objects or concepts). Contemporary art should be used to expand their ideas and help them explore media and processes. Never be reluctant to use a work of art because you think your pupils might not understand it. Just by looking at and exploring it, they will absorb ideas and information and be able to learn from it.

You may be surprised that your students understand more than you expected. Allow them time to look and consider without explaining, then let them tell you what they think a work is about.

Working with contemporary art often provides opportunities for open-ended projects, which in turn allows students to take more responsibility and control. It helps pupils of all ages to see art in a different way. It can be daunting to actively encourage the application of new technologies if these are new areas to you, but if you accept the need for support (from students, ICT technicians, local printers or graphic artists, for instance) then you will find that you can use contemporary media with confidence and success. Some suggestions for expanding students' understanding and usage of contemporary art (all exercises are suitable for all year groups, depending on how you adapt and modify them) are available online.

Expectations and progression 2

In general, during Key Stage (KS) 3, art teachers are responsible for assessing pupils' work based on the National Curriculum. After 14, when art students have elected to take the subject to a higher level, the external criteria of the examination boards take over. Judgements about how to mark and record progress at KS3 are made by individual art departments in the context of the needs of the school, department and achievements of pupils.

Assessment for learning (AfL)

AfL has become a significant part of effective teaching and learning, especially since the publication of Black and Wiliam's research in 1998, which produced evidence to support the use of formative assessment processes to enhance students' performance. Rather than simply finding out what they've learned, as in summative assessment (or assessment of learning), formative assessment (or AfL) focuses on providing information to help pupils improve their overall performance.

The main factor of AfL is in making sure that students understand how and why they are being assessed and using assessment in the classroom to raise their achievement. It is based on the idea that pupils improve most when they understand what they are meant to be learning and how they can do it; you need to use self-assessment techniques to help them understand where and how they need to improve. In this way, AfL aims to ensure that assessment is an integral part of all teaching and learning. Students learn best when they understand what they are trying to learn and what is expected of them; they are given feedback about the quality of their work and what they can do to improve; and they are involved in deciding what needs to be done next and who can help them if they need it. It is important therefore to regularly monitor students' progress and refer to assessment criteria so students understand your expectations. Make sure that all students understand both the particular learning objectives for each lesson and the longer term objectives that you want them to learn over an entire project. Structure your objectives so that learning is the focus, not the outcome, product or technique (although these will be essential to the learning). Here are a few ideas for implementing AfL:

- *Peer marking*: Pupils give their work to a friend who marks it against a checklist of learning objectives. It's their responsibility to make sure everything is in order before giving it to you for marking.
- *Class gallery*: Near the end of the lesson, students walk around the class looking at each other's work. Then they choose a piece to feed back on, describing its strengths and weaknesses.
- *Reading marked work*: Give everyone a short time during lessons to look at marked work, so they have an opportunity to absorb and respond to your feedback.
- *Grades*: Don't always provide grades when marking work as students often focus on them without then wanting to find out how they can improve. To counteract this, write only comments, showing them where and how they can improve.
- *No hands up*: When asking the class questions, insist on a 'no hands up' rule to give everyone essential thinking time to prepare a response before you choose someone to ask.
- *Traffic light cards*: Give every pupil a red, yellow and green card. If a pupil shows his or her yellow card, it means you are going too fast. If someone wants to ask a question, he or she holds up a red card. You can then choose someone showing green or yellow to answer.

Often a brief word as pupils are working has a great effect. They then have the opportunity to ask questions and give you the chance to make further suggestions.

◆ Marking

Try to keep a balance and organize how you mark and how often you do it. Some people find marking a bit over several days works, while others prefer to mark a large amount in one chunk. If you find you are drowning in marking, refer to your departmental policy and make sure that you are keeping to school and parents' expectations of marking frequency.

There are a number of ways that you can help yourself. Often electronic mark sheets mean you can simply enter grades or percentages and the system works out what level each pupil is working at. By keeping a regular record of students' marks, you will be able to see where they have made progress and where they need to improve. Colour coding students' data can be extremely useful in giving you an instant overall view of how an individual or entire class is performing and where there are weaknesses. However you record this, make a note for yourself about the type of activity and where, if any, individuals are excelling or struggling. Tracking sheets are extremely helpful – these can be actual sheets on which you write or spreadsheets on the computer. They should contain areas where students should be making progress and titles of projects or units.

In addition, by keeping all pupils informed about your assessment procedure throughout the process of making, appraisal and modification, they will develop a propensity for autonomous learning, which will help them to make judgements for themselves and be able to adapt and improve their own work independently. In turn, this helps with self-motivation, even as the subject becomes more demanding.

◆ Level descriptions and tracking pupils' progress

At the end of a unit of work, year or KS, you will need to work out how students are doing in comparison with national standards. The National Curriculum requires all students to reach particular levels and levels in art at KS3 are assessed against descriptions by each pupil's art teacher on the basis of what they have achieved in either two or three years (depending on individual school's policies about KS3). Assessing your pupils in this way gives you, other teachers in the school, parents and pupils an indication of each pupil's performance in relation to others of a comparable age within the school and throughout the country. It is useful to set a test for pupils at the beginning of Year 7 and apply the same test at the end of Year 9. Roughly speaking, you can usually predict where a child will be by the end of Year 9 if you do this. If pupils attain 4c in Year 7, by the end of Year 9 the same pupils should reach between 5c and 5a. If they attain 4a in Year 7, by the end of Year 9 they should reach 6c, 6b or 6a. If in Year 7 they achieve 5b, by the end of Year 9 it is predicted that they will achieve 7c, 7b or 7a and if at the end of Year 7 they accomplish 6c, two years later, they should reach 8c, 8b or 8c.

Progress in art is measured as students' skills and understanding develop. Being art, however, this is not as straightforward as answering questions correctly. You will have to see evidence in a wide range of skills and abilities for each pupil to reach certain levels. Ensure that all your pupils understand exactly what is meant by each level; how they have reached it and what they could do to get an even higher level. At the end of KS3, you will judge which level description best fits each pupil's performance.

When making a judgement, you will have to take into account strengths and weaknesses across a range of projects over two or three years. A single piece of work will not cover everything, although it will provide partial evidence of attainment in one or more aspects of a level description. Comparing several pieces of work will enable you to make a judgement about which level best fits a pupil's overall performance.

It follows that in planning projects you will need to provide opportunities for pupils to display their progress in various ways, such as: using a variety of media in practical work; participating in discussion; analyzing and evaluating in written work; and working with a partner or in groups. This is something that becomes easier with practise. The criteria for levels include practical skills (media, manipulation, scale and so on), contextual analysis, evaluation and exploration of images, all of which can vary vastly. Pupils are assessed on their use of a range of materials, understanding of images and their ability to respond creatively to a given problem. For your first couple of years doing this, work with another art teacher in order to learn how these achievements should be awarded. Meanwhile, if you concentrate on helping your KS3 students learn skills that will help their progress in Year 11 and consequently in Years 12 and 13, you will be moving in the right direction.

◆ Effective learning

For effective learning to take place, pupils need to understand what they are meant to be achieving so it is vital for you to have a clear sense of how each of your lessons will allow pupils to progress. For every project, make sure that you are clear about what objectives and tasks you will be insisting upon and that you have prioritized outcomes and activities. It is all too easy, especially when you are new to teaching, to focus on what you will teach, rather than what you expect pupils to learn. There is a difference!

It is vitally important how you apply learning objectives and ensure your pupils achieve them. Always make sure that everyone you are teaching knows the criteria you are following to assess their work. With older students, criteria for success are predetermined in the assessment objectives, but from 11–14, by inviting pupils to participate in decisions about goals and what they will be assessed on, you will help them understand why they are learning. Explain what, why and how they need to learn and then see if they can formulate some sensible criteria for assessment. Whether you do this or not, at the start of each lesson when you write your objectives on the board, make sure that everyone can make connections between these and the criteria for assessment.

Lesson objectives should always be directly measurable through assessment, so make sure your criteria specifically measure whether the objectives were reached or not. Always explain the objectives in terms of what pupils will learn rather than what they will do. In other words, what they will get out of a particular task or project. Use appropriate language to ensure that they understand it all, introducing any significant vocabulary.

◆ Constant assessment

Art in general allows for more of a personal approach to assessment and much of what teachers and pupils do in classrooms can be classed as appraisal. By observing pupils at their tasks and responding to your questions, you are constantly assessing their knowledge, understanding and skills. These are an essential part of everyday classroom practice and are all part of AfL. Whether it is a passing comment or a written report, any assessment process should be sensitive and constructive, aimed to boost students' confidence and enthusiasm. So when giving feedback on areas for development, make sure it is practical and positive, such as:

- 'You are developing some mature skills in observational drawing, but try to keep your pencil sharp, press lightly and keep focused in order to build on your promising skills.'
- 'When applying paint to paper, keep it to a creamy consistency. If it becomes too runny, as has happened in areas of your painting, blot with paper towel and mix more paint using less water.'
- 'By improving your powers of concentration, you could achieve

more each lesson and show off more of your understanding of colour and harmony.'

Art and design teachers tend to want to share their wide range of conceptual, critical and technical skills and their enthusiasm for the subject as well as their high expectations of pupils. Sometimes, however, you need to withhold your input and let your pupils find things out for themselves. In this way, you will give them the tools to develop their own abilities in critical reflection. Stepping back occasionally will also give you a chance to consider how you will challenge everyone, sustain their interests and identify clear learning objectives.

◆ *Suggestions for effective learning and assessment (KS3)*

- If space allows, it's a good idea for every pupil to have his or her own folder of work. They must name and date everything they do and keep their folders organized and tidy.
- If you do not have space for individual folders, try having class folders or drawers where everyone keeps their work. Again, pupils are to take responsibility for this – keeping their own work organized, up to date and neat.
- Give regular feedback to everyone, whether oral or written, making sure you keep written records.
- Always keep your feedback positive, encouraging and constructive.
- During or at the end of each topic or project, all pupils should assess their own work.
- Before you appraise their work, give all pupils your criteria for assessment or engage them to help you decide on the criteria.
- To share ideas about criteria, give everyone a small piece of paper. On it they should write suggestions and put the paper in a box. During the lesson, everyone takes out a piece of paper, reads it and writes their opinions on the back.
- Whatever criteria pupils come up with, make it clear to them that you have the final say, as it always has to adhere to the requirements of the National Curriculum.
- Criteria should be based on end of KSstatements.
- Divide the class into pairs. Partners should group with another pair and give feedback on each other's work.

For positive appraisals, include constructive vocabulary, such as:

* explore * investigate * develop * create * analyze * evaluate * modify * adapt *

Self-assessment

It is extremely important that every student feels completely involved in the creative process. They need to understand that their input leads to greater ownership of their work. By involving them in the decision making process from the start, their expressiveness and coherence will increase. Even when you might prefer to retain control, try to hold back and encourage input from students. This is valuable for their development. In a similar way, self-assessment is important for students at all levels of secondary education. By assessing their own work, they become empowered, taking greater responsibility for and so ownership of their work.

It is important students learn how to assess their own work, recognize the levels they are aiming for and how they can progress. To help them gain skills in self-assessment from the start of their time at secondary school, build on their understanding, analytical skills and specialist vocabulary. Integrate methods of analyzing work – their own and others – in your lessons and always provide a list of appropriate art terms for KS3, 4 and 5. Self-assessment should become a regular activity and you should give all students opportunities to assess themselves during and/or after a project. (Self-assessment should be part of the process of GCSE and A level evaluation and annotation, buy does not necessarily need to be given as a separate procedure. Having said this, there is a sample self-assessment sheet for GCSE and A level, available online). Students should expect to assess their own work so early on in their time with you, you might find it helpful to take them through the self-assessment process that you are instigating. Although by doing this, the first task that they self-assess will not be a true self-assessment, it will help individuals to build the skills and confidence necessary to continue doing this and benefiting from it. Tell students to be thoughtful and constructive rather than overly self-effacing. Here are some suggested formats you could use:

1. *SWAT:* self-assessment can be as basic as a SWAT page, divided into four in pupils' sketchbooks drawn at the end of each project:

Strengths .*(What have I done that has worked well?)*	Weaknesses .*(What do I need to change/could I have improved?)*
Achievements .*(What did I try out that was new to me or ambitious?)*	Teacher's comments

Self-assessment sheet (1) Expectations and progression

Name: LEVEL 4	Form/group: LEVEL 5	Project title: LEVEL 6	Term: LEVEL 7	Date: LEVEL 8
I have looked at and considered a variety of ideas	I have shown that I have researched relevant ideas and sources	I have researched ideas and sources, explaining how and why it is relevant to my own work	I have carefully researched and assessed several ideas and sources that are relevant to my work	I have thoroughly investigated and assessed a wide and relevant range and selection of ideas and sources
I have compared the work of some different artists and made useful comments about them	I have considered, understood and explained some of the ideas, meanings and methods of certain artists	I have understood, explained and clearly analysed some ideas, meanings and methods of artists who are relevant to my work	I have analysed and commented on the work of relevant artists, showing understanding of their styles, ideas, meanings and methods	I have thoroughly understood, examined and commented on the ideas, styles, ideas, meanings and methods of artists who are relevant to my work
I have experimented with some ideas, modifying my work as I progress	I have experimented with ideas and methods, modifying and improving my work as I progress	I have compared my work to the work of other artists and have experimented, adapted and improved it as a result	I have understood the ideas and methods of other artists, which has helped me to take creative risks as I develop and adapt my own work	I have used my understanding of the ideas and methods of other artists to take imaginative risks with my own creative ideas and work
I have used materials carefully to produce a final piece	I have made good use of materials to reach a thoughtful and controlled final piece	I have used materials and creative techniques effectively and consistently to produce a competent final piece	I have shown consistently thoughtful and imaginative use of materials and creative techniques to produce a confident final piece	I have expressed ideas clearly, using materials and techniques confidently and imaginatively, producing a mature, original and meaningful final piece
My comments about what I did well:	My comments about what I need to improve:	Teacher's comments about what I did well:	Teacher's comments about what I need to improve:	Teacher's mark:

Self-assessment sheet (2)

Name:　　　Form/group:　　　Date:　　　Art teacher:　　　Project title:

For each question, tick the relevant boxes and explain in words in the space

1. Did I complete all my work to the best of my ability?
Yes ☐
Not fully ☐
No ☐

2. Did I complete my work in the given time limit?
Yes ☐
Not fully ☐
No ☐

3. Did I concentrate at all times during lessons?
Yes ☐
Not fully ☐
No ☐

4. Have I fulfilled all the aims and objectives for this project?
Yes ☐
Not fully ☐
No ☐

5. Did I try out different ways of doing things?
Yes ☐
Not fully ☐
No ☐

6. Did I find out significant information to back up my creative ideas?
Yes ☐
Not fully ☐
No ☐

7. Did I stretch myself when trying out new materials or skills?
Yes ☐
Not fully ☐
No ☐

8. Are there aspects of this work that I am proud of?
Yes ☐
Not fully ☐
No ☐

9. Are there aspects of this work that I am not proud of?
Yes ☐
Not fully ☐
No ☐

10. What have I learned and what could I have improved?

Out of 10 for achievement and effort, what would you give yourself?
Achievement ☐　Effort ☐

Teacher's grade:
Achievement ☐　Effort ☐
Teacher's comments:

Self-assessment sheet (3)

What have I learned about myself during this project?	Name: Form: Date:
	What did I do that helped me to learn?
How did I do? Did I produce the best work I could, or if not, what could I have done to improve?	What did I learn?
	What did someone else do to help me to learn this? (This could be a teacher or someone in your class)
How do I feel at the end of the project? Why?	How did I feel during the project? Did that affect my progress? What might have helped?

or give them a more complex printed sheet: (see Self-assessment sheet (1))
You could use something in between the two (see Self-assessment sheet (2))
or see Self-assessment sheet (3).

2.. *Exercise books*: special art department exercise books. Pupils are responsible for keeping these neat, well ordered and for bringing them to every art lesson. Every fourth page should be left blank for your comments. Exercise books should be handed in at the end of each project with the practical work.

3.. *Diaries*: chronological records of work in progress and reviews of work completed.

4.. *Scrap books*: an informal collection of images used for inspiration, pieces of information, notes on work and photos.

5.. *Sketchbooks*: similar to scrap books, also including a compilation of the development of ideas including text, photos and other images, plans and thoughts.

In order to promote the climate of self-assessment, encourage students to ask questions during lessons. Maintain their confidence to do this by asking them plenty of open questions. Open questions encourage students to think independently and are less confrontational. Sample open questions you might use during lessons include:

- Does this work remind you of anything – if so, what and why?
- What do you think the artist intended us to think when looking at the work?
- How will you go about solving that problem?
- What made you choose that colour?
- What information can you share about that technique?
- What would you do differently next time?
- What do you see?
- How does it make you feel?

Measuring your expectations

A reliable method of categorizing the levels of your students' learning skills is Bloom's taxonomy, which the educational psychiatrist Benjamin Bloom created in 1956 with a team of educational psychiatrists. Many educators follow Bloom's tax-onomy to measure students' work and raise standards. It's a useful tool as long as you don't allow it to become time consuming. It's a classification of learning objectives that are all about building on knowledge and helping your students to apply, analyze, synthesize and evaluate – particularly pertinent to art.

Bloom and his team found that over 95 per cent of test questions that students encounter require them to simply recall information. So they divided learning objectives into three 'domains', stating that if teachers focused on all three domains they would create a more holistic and rounded form of education. The three domains are: affective, psychomotor and cognitive. *Affective* objectives target awareness and development in pupils' attitudes and emotional responses. *Psychomotor* objectives usually focus on development and progress in behaviour or skills. The *cognitive* domain is the main part of the taxonomy, as traditional education tends to emphasize skills in this domain. Bloom divided the cognitive domain into six parts. Cognitive objectives usually focus on knowledge, comprehension and thinking through problems.

During the 1990s, Bloom's taxonomy was updated by Lorin Anderson and another group of psychologists, testing and assessment specialists and curriculum theorists, to make it more relevant for twenty-first century students and teachers. The revised taxonomy was published in 2001. It includes changes in three broad categories: terminology, structure and emphasis (see table below).

Old version	New version
1. Evaluation	Creating
2. Synthesis	Evaluating
3. Analysis	Analyzing
4. Application	Applying
5. Comprehension	Understanding
6. Knowledge	Remembering

Here are ways you might use the taxonomy to ensure pupils are learning holistically:

1. *Remembering/knowledge*: To see whether students have gained specific information, ask questions that include any of the words: list, name, order, recognize, relate, recall and repeat.
2. *Understanding/comprehension*: To test students' abilities to interpret facts, for example showing that they understand why each artist

worked in his or her particular style, questioning could include: contrast, describe, discuss, explain, express, identify, indicate, locate, recognize, review, select and interpret.

3. *Applying/application*: To ensure that students are implementing knowledge they have learned, include the following in your questions: examine, illustrate, show, apply, choose, demonstrate, interpret, practice, sketch, use and write.

4. *Analyzing/analysis*: Students at this level should show that they understand how to analyze and differentiate problems. Questioning could include: explain, investigate, analyze, appraise, categorize, compare, contrast, criticize, differentiate, discriminate, distinguish, examine and experiment.

5. *Evaluating/synthesis*: Students are required to take a problem, make judgements and make something out of them. Questions to test this objective include: plan, invent, imagine, create, compose, arrange, assemble, collect, construct, design, develop, formulate, manage and organize.

6. *Creating/evaluation*: This is the highest level of Bloom's taxonomy, where students are expected to assess information and to put elements together to form a coherent or functional solution through planning and producing. Questions to test that your students are doing this well include: select, appraise, argue, assess, choose, compare, defend, judge, predict, support and evaluate.

◆ Learning styles

In addition to ways of moving students through phases of progress, it is important to understand the ways in which individuals learn. Scientists have identified a variety of different learning styles related to different areas of the human brain. While everyone uses combinations of these, we each have a preferred learning style that we naturally use when trying to understand new or complex information. The learning styles or intelligences include:

- linguistic – the ability to write or speak fluently
- logical – the ability to deal with numbers
- visual/spatial – the ability to visualize or imagine
- musical – the ability to keep rhythm
- physical – the ability to move well (this can be the whole body or simply fingers and hands)
- social – the ability to communicate well
- intra-personal – the ability to analyze and perceive the self clearly
- naturalist – the ability to recognize and live in harmony with nature

In differentiation, all teachers are expected to take special measures to ensure that all students are given opportunities to learn using the styles that suit them best. Art lessons are particularly suited to a variety of learning styles and methods and you can use this to improve the way you teach. You can set the same tasks for all abilities, modifying your expectations for students with differing aptitudes, or you can set different activities for students of varying abilities, perhaps with a range of tasks and activities to choose from. These could vary in complexity, learning methods, format and materials or the ways in which they learn. Dr Vernon Magnesen of the University of Texas found that the percentage of what we remember changes depending on the activity:

- reading – 20 per cent recall
- listening/hearing – 30 per cent recall
- looking/seeing – 40 per cent recall
- speaking/saying – 50 per cent recall
- doing – 60 per cent recall
- seeing, saying, hearing and doing – 90 per cent recall.

Evidence, if ever there was, that all art lessons should use multisensory learning techniques! (see Lesson plan for Year 9 on p. 35).

◆ *Encouraging positive attitudes*

To encourage your pupils to be constructive and diligent in your lessons, always consider *how* rather than solely *what* you will teach. All learning is affected by state of mind, so you need to get the group or class into an enthusiastic mindset. Simply ignore any lassitude or negative attitudes, unless individuals are affecting others and then this should be dealt with promptly. Often those who draw attention to themselves simply need some positive attention and be made to feel as valued as the more able in the class. With art, there is always something to interest everyone, so if your projects, activities and lessons are varied enough, you should always be able to engage everyone.

During lessons, continually monitor progress by asking questions and moving about the room to check on work being produced. It is important to give feedback as you do this, either collectively to the class (what they should be achieving) or individually. Make sure that this is quick and constructive so pupils can decide for themselves whether or not they are

Lesson plan for Year 9

Timing	Teacher activities and resources	Pupil learning activities/responses
15 minutes	**Introduction:** PowerPoint of Pop Art works. (Any, but include Richard Hamilton's 'Just What is it that Makes Today's Homes so Different, so Appealing?' Teacher-led discussion about the work: why did they do it? What did it mean? Was it worth it? Does it make sense? What inspired them? Was it the first time that art was allowed to be fun? What do they think the establishment thought of it?	Looking Listening Speaking/responding
35 minutes	**Main lesson:** Selection of magazines, wrappers and other packaging. Glue, scissors, pencils, charcoal, paint and felt tips. Sheets of A2 or A3 paper. Discuss what they would do if they were Pop artists working today. How would they interpret Richard Hamilton's 'Just What is it that Makes Today's Homes so Different, so Appealing?' Individually, they are to make their own version during this lesson.	Considering, selecting, planning Discussing Modifying Technical skills: understanding scale and balance Creativity; use of imagination, colour and paint
10 minutes	**Plenary:** Select some students to present their work to the rest of the class, explaining why they included the elements they did and what their thinking was behind their work. Encourage the rest of the class to ask questions and to give their opinions about each other's work.	Speaking, communication and presentation Considering and critiquing Expressing and sharing ideas and thoughts Discussing Looking Listening
30 minutes	**Homework:** Find out about Pop art and what it meant. Write a paragraph explaining the concepts behind it.	Reading Researching Writing

progressing correctly. Give feedback on as wide a variety of issues as possible, such as art techniques, finding relevant artists or artefacts, ways to improve attentiveness and understanding or how to boost a lack of self-confidence, for example. A few further ideas to help you promote enthusiasm and sustain motivation in your lessons are given online.

Attainment targets

In order to achieve the highest attainment, students need to be encouraged to experiment and take risks – but only once they have mastered the necessary and traditional skills. Within a 'normal' school timetable, the allocation for art lessons at KS3 and 4 is not conducive to extremely ambitious work. While painting, drawing, some print and 3D work can be fitted into most schemes of work, large installations and highly evolved technical projects do not 'slot in' comfortably. Most art teachers are keen to encourage students to experiment and work with new materials and concepts, but these are often difficult to accommodate. There are already so many demands on teachers' time that unless you can manage to fit in gifted and talented or enrichment days or run after school clubs and workshops, stretching resources to encompass ambitious projects is probably best left for KS4 and 5. On the subject of attainment, consider whom your attainment targets are for: you, the teacher; the department; the school; individual students; or the authorities? Once you are clear about this, each time you assess be mindful of for whom you are assessing. This will help you evaluate the general usefulness of your methods.

◆ Suggestions for reflection

By giving students guidelines, they will have the chance to reflect, modify and improve their work. Give them an outline of your expectations at the start of a project. Any time they have a moment, such as when, inevitably, some pupils rush their work and think they've finished early, they should be referred back to these. Remind students to regularly check these expectations to make sure they are meeting them. You could also give a list of questions at the start of each project to reflect on throughout it.

◆ *Suggested questions*

- How organized is my work?
- How informed is my research?
- Have I used a variety of materials and explained why?
- Is there a plan for my final piece?
- What do I need to do to improve?
- How skilful is my drawing?
- Have I used primary and secondary sources?
- Have I responded to other artists?
- What other artists have I responded to?
- How do I feel about my piece of work?
- What have I learned through creating my piece of work?
- What has worked well? Why?
- What would I improve? Why?

◆ *Raise achievement*

As we know, art gives pupils with different skills and aptitudes opportunities to achieve success. Make the most of this by creating a positive environment and providing a broad range of projects using a diverse range of visual materials to stimulate interest and generate ideas. Encourage all pupils to look, consider, listen and discuss; to challenge assumptions, develop their investigative skills and explore complex issues and ideas. Always explain the importance of keeping an open mind, of taking risks and of recognizing that there is no one correct answer for artistic problems.

When possible, invite artists into the school, whether painters, sculptors, illustrators, ceramicists or model-makers. Professional artists stimulate students' minds and give them fresh ideas and expectations. Also take them on art related trips – to local areas or to art galleries. By stimulating your pupils' imaginations, they will produce fresh ideas, which will help to raise achievement, improve their attitudes to learning and their behaviour.

Appraising yourself

Finally, don't forget to regularly appraise yourself and how your teaching is going. This may sound unnecessary with all the other demands on your time, but it will help you to improve and develop the quality of your teaching. This is nothing to do with being observed or official self-evaluation, but an informal way that you can help yourself. About once a term, ask yourself some frank questions, such as:

- How well do I plan my lessons? Are they structured clearly and coherently with logical targets?
- Do lessons feed comfortably into each other, with activities that help students build on their knowledge, understanding and skills?
- Am I well organized? Do I have materials and equipment ready for each lesson?
- Are my explanations understandable and succinct enough for each age group and do I inspire – or bore?
- Do I engage all pupils and do I employ both open and closed questions?
- Do I vary activities and pace during each lesson?
- Do I maintain a level of control and respect in lessons that encourages learning?
- Do I give regular feedback and advice to all my students?
- Do I mark work regularly, constructively and supportively?
- Do I need to brush up on any aspects of my subject knowledge, practical skills or theoretical understanding?

The overall aim of this self-evaluation is to determine what went well, what went badly, how much students have learned and what you need to work on for them to improve. Another method of self-assessment is to assess the whole department (see the assessment chart on the following page).

By reflecting critically on both your teaching and your students' learning, you will see where improvements need to be made. This is one of the keys to making progress and improving the ways in which you teach.

Assessment			
Tick the boxes that are relevant to your department			
Do your assessments match these criteria?	Fully in place	Partly in place	Not in place
Assessment is *for* learning, not *of* learning. It is used to guide lesson planning and identify the particular help that individuals and groups of pupils need.			
Whole classes or groups of pupils have curricular targets for improvement, drawn from objectives from the scheme of work. Individual targets for pupils with SEN are incorporated in IEPs.			
There is a system for tracking pupils' progress against their targets and for responding to pupils who fall behind.			
Marking includes teachers' comments which show clearly what a pupil needs to do to improve. A response from pupils is expected.			
Records are manageable and useful for teachers. Individual records and pupil targets are kept for pupils whose progress is distinctly different from the average.			
Pupil self-assessment is expected and used as part of the assessment record.			
List three action points to improve assessment.			

Planning

If there is one thing you need to do well as an art teacher, it is planning and organizing yourself and others! Good planning is essential for effective art teaching, making sure that students cover the curriculum thoroughly and well, making good progress. The more organized you are with planning and structuring your lessons, the easier your job will be and the more confident you will become. Effective lesson planning consists of three main considerations:

- general aims and specific outcomes of lessons
- the most effective learning environment and activities
- monitoring and evaluation of pupils' progress to assess the success of lessons.

When writing schemes of work (SoW), don't forget the age group you are teaching. What motivates a 14 or 15 year old, for instance, is a different consideration to what inspires an 11 year old.

Meeting curriculum requirements

In order to differentiate between your pupils and to meet most curriculum requirements, sufficient planning is imperative. Some art departments share SoW, with all teachers in the department following them at the same time. This makes sense; if pupils have different teachers in subsequent years, they will still have covered the same objectives and learned comparable skills. Other departments encourage teachers to devise their own individual SoW. Again, as long as the skills applied are similar, this also works. If you plan thoroughly, you will reduce your workload considerably. Here is a table showing the National Curriculum levels and skills that pupils should know by the end of Key Stage (KS) 3:

National Curriculum Art	Level 1	Level 2	Level 3	Level 4	Level 5	Level 6	Level 7	Level 8	Exceptional Performance
Exploring and developing ideas	Respond to ideas	Explore ideas	Explore ideas and collect information for work	Explore and collect ideas. Research to help development	Explore ideas and select information. Make use of research, taking account of purpose	Explore and assess ideas and information. Take account of purpose and audience in development	Analyse, assess and organize ideas and information. Develop ideas and meanings in visual and other ways	Evaluate relevance of ideas, including beliefs and conventions. Research, document and present ideas appropriately.	Initiate research, critically evaluate ideas. Respond to new possibilities, identify different interpretations and analyse ideas in relation to purpose
Investigating and making	Use materials and processes to communicate ideas, make images and artefacts	Investigate a variety of materials and processes communicate ideas and design and make images and artefacts	Investigate qualities in materials and processes. Design and make for different purposes	Use knowledge of materials and processes to make artefacts and images that suit intentions	Manipulate materials and processes to match intentions	Manipulate materials and processes and analyse outcomes. Intentions are realized	Interpret visual and tactile qualities. Increasing independence in development of ideas and meanings to realize intentions	Make use of potential of materials and processes. Sustain investigations and exploit visual characteristics	Exploit characteristics of materials and processes. Sustain investigations to fully realize intentions
Evaluating and developing work	Describe thoughts and feelings about own and others' work	Comment on differences in others' work and suggest ways of improving own	Comment on similarities and differences in others' work, adapting and improving own	Compare and comment on methods and approaches in relation to context	Analyse and comment on the approaches in your own work and the work of others in relation to context	Analyse and comment on ideas and meanings in your own work and the work of others. Explain how context affects practice	Analyse and explain the contexts of their own and others' work	Evaluate contexts; articulate differences in views and practice. Show insights gained from the work of others	Identify the reasons for different interpretations of ideas and meanings. Clearly communicate views and insights

◆ *Allow for flexibility*

Planning, recording and reviewing SoW and individual lessons are key requirements of teaching. There is no set way of doing this. Some teachers record the content, resources and methods they will use in their lessons in detail, others simply list activities they will include. Whatever your method, planning shouldn't be too rigid as you need to be flexible and allow for unexpected eventualities. Planning is essential, however, to give you the security of structure and a set of objectives for each lesson. If possible, try mind mapping your ideas with others in your department. Newly qualified and very experienced teachers often find benefits in pooling and discussing ideas. New ideas and materials should be tried out.

Consider pace, pitch and variety and make sure that your aims are suitable for the age group, areas they have already covered, their abilities and what they are working towards. Avoid repetitive or predictable lessons: each starter and plenary should vary as much as the central activity. Don't always assume that pace means diving into the main activity as soon as possible. Often, spending time trying out materials and methods encourages more varied and creative responses. Make sure that you are an expert at any techniques or with materials that you will be introducing in lessons.

◆ *Planning tips*

Before you begin planning SoW and lessons, you must consider pupils' progression and how you want them to develop, i.e. think of the end result you want first. Consider whole class learning objectives as well as individual needs. If in doubt when initially planning, think about content, materials and activities. Bear in mind what your pupils already know:

- Where are they now in terms of knowledge, understanding and skills?
- Is any revision of previous work needed?
- Are concepts, resources and tasks you will be covering suitable for the age and range of your pupils' prior achievements and abilities?
- Do your lessons build on achievements and challenges of earlier lessons?
- At the end of each lesson, what new knowledge, understanding and skills do you want pupils to have gained (i.e. the lesson objectives)?
- On what will you base your assessment criteria?

- What new vocabulary will you be introducing and how?
- What teaching methods will best meet your objectives? (For example individual, paired or group work.)
- What resources will you require?
- How will you distribute materials and organize tidying and clearing up at the end of the lesson?
- What will the timings of each activity or parts of the lesson be?
- How will you sustain pupils' interests throughout the lesson?
- How will you help your pupils to engage with the work of others?
- How will you differentiate to suit individual needs?
- In what ways will you cater for special educational needs pupils, from less able to gifted and talented?
- Will you offer extension work? If so, how will you make it sufficiently challenging without involving new knowledge?
- Will you set a complementary or additional homework task? At what point in the lesson will you instruct pupils about this?

Your plenary should reinforce and re-establish your learning objectives. This makes it clear for you and students what has been successful and what has not. Keep the relevant lesson plan handy throughout each lesson. Highlighting important points will remind you at a glance of essential things. On the following pages are three different examples of functional lesson planning sheets. Many schools have their own recommended lesson planning formats, but the following provide workable structures should you need them.

One of the most difficult areas to plan for is when some students race through the tasks you have set and finish early (whether successfully or not), and conversely when others do not complete their work within a given time limit. This is where extension activities or clarifying the learning objectives and assessment criteria are invaluable.

Long and medium term planning

If your department does not teach the same SoW at the same time then ideally you should sit down with colleagues in the department and list what each year group should cover. Planning in this way will make sure that all pupils across a year group experience a similar programme of study, particularly one that encourages progress from year to year. It's handy to do this, towards the end of the academic year in preparation for the next.

Blank lesson planning sheet (1)

Date:_____ Period:_____ Class:_____ Scheme of Work reference:_____ Teacher:_____

Resources required:

Background/context:

Aims and expectations of lesson/curricular objectives:

Proposed activities:

End of lesson/ plenary / feedback from pupils providing evidence of learning:

Homework:

Lesson planning sheet (2)

Teacher: Period: Date: Exam/Key Stage: Class: Level/grade:

Title of project: Week of project: Number of weeks of entire project: Lesson topic:

Background/context: *(E.g. Pupils have studied... and practised techniques for... They have explored... and produced their own...)*

Learning objectives:
By the end of the lesson, all pupils should be able to:
Most pupils should be able to:
Some pupils should be able to:

Assessment: *(Add features of assessment relevant to the lesson)*

Resources: *(List resources needed)*

Teaching strategies:
Mind mapping	ICT	Practical investigation	Visit
Group discussion	Individual work	Problem solving	Role play
Group work	Lecture	DVD/interactive whiteboard	Design/make

Learning skills:
Comprehension	Listening	Personal/social	Problem solving
Empathizing	ICT	Research skills	Analysis
Citizenship	Information handling	Observing	Understanding of materials

Homework:

Provision for different learning rates: *(Differentiation)*

Student information: *(Identify any SENs or G&T pupils in this particular class or group)*

Blank lesson planning sheet (3)

Teacher:	Date:	Number of pupils:	Number of SEN pupils:
Year group:	Lesson number in SoW:	Period:	SEN conditions:
Learning Objectives:	Resources:	Key vocabulary:	Homework:

Teaching / learning	Pupil activities
Introduction/starter:	
Main lesson:	
Plenary:	
Differentiation:	Assessment:

Long term planning usually works around the school calendar and available resources. It should help you to keep focused on the main learning outcomes for specific schemes of work and how they fit into the overall picture of students' progress and development.

For long term planning, take a large sheet of paper – A2 or A3 – and list, mind map, draw flowcharts or diagrams to work out what you would like each year group to learn and what skills or resources you will need for that to happen. Note how one particular skill might lead on to another or how the study of a certain group of artists could perhaps help to inform pupils about something else. Try to build on these links and connections. In addition, consider your department's areas of expertise and incorporate these where possible. Before you begin, establish what you are required to cover or what the heads of department or faculty want you to cover. Half-termly or termly art projects work particularly well in most secondary schools at KS3, but some schools where there is a particularly mixed level of abilities need to introduce three or four fresh projects each term. To maintain the interest and enthusiasm of your 11–14 year olds, introduce new aspects of each theme during each project. While lesson planning is usually an individual pursuit, long term planning needs to be a team effort to ensure that everyone in the department agrees on strategies.

Once you have planned ahead in this way, you need to plan in slightly more detail for the medium term. Whether or not this includes individual lesson plans, it should always comprise learning objectives and key outcomes. You need both long and medium term planning so that you can teach each lesson with a clear understanding of where you are heading and when you intend to reach your goal. In this way, you will be able to visualize where you will be with your different groups at particular junctures in the year and projects that will engender inspiring and striking display material.

It's also important to plan for when you might take classes into the ICT rooms; when you will incorporate visits to galleries or other sites; when you might not be able to teach in your usual room; or when you might not be able to teach your class (such as when you are absent, invigilating other art exams or on a visit with another class). Medium term planning is useful for working out how you will differentiate and what resources you need to order or find in advance. This should lead on to the SoW and, in turn, to your lesson plans.

◆ Schemes of Work

SoW should be detailed enough for individual art teachers to interpret them in ways that are most beneficial to their particular set of learners. QCA's recommended SoW are simply suggestions for teachers to follow and do not have to be adhered to. If you create your own SoW thoughtfully and carefully, you will save yourself a great deal of work over the following year. Learning objectives should be central to your SoW planning. Always consider what learning has occurred and what progression you wish your pupils to make. Include in each SoW the content, methods and resources as well as any pace and variety of learning styles that you will need. Be careful that your ideas are not repetitive or predictable and there is enough scope to make each lesson sufficiently different and interesting, yet still fulfil the needs of individual learners.

SoW should be updated regularly to make sure they carry on being appropriate and relevant. They can be produced in a range of formats. From KS4, lesson plans should be based on the syllabus for the relevant qualification (i.e. GCSE or A level). On the following two pages are some examples of SoW for KS3, some adhering to QCA suggestions and some moving in slightly different directions, but always emphasizing the important skills that children aged 11–14 should be developing.

◆ Effective planning

One of the challenges of effective lesson planning is preparing and delivering learning activities that closely match the needs and abilities of different students in every class you teach. All activities must promote aspects of knowledge, understanding and skills as well as maintaining the interest and motivation of pupils. Effective lesson plans are not too long and detailed, but they should include: clear objectives and structure; approximate timings; differentiation; homework; required resources; key vocabulary; skills and activities.

◆ Constraints

If one hour a week is allocated for art and design at KS3 and you add in days when pupils are ill or off-timetable for various other reasons, most only have about 30 hours of art lessons a year. At KS4, art lessons take up about 2.5 hours a week, but again with absences for illness, school trips and other school events, the

Scheme of work

Year group: 9	Project – icons	Aims – understand elements of successful composition and make connections with artists' work and contemporary images, using compositional skills to enhance visual impact and meaning.	Objectives – produce an image of a contemporary icon, using mixed media and compositional skills to create something meaningful and enduring.
Lesson number 1	**Skill development** Recognition of elements of composition and what makes a stable or dynamic composition.	**Activity/resources** Look at a variety of paintings and discuss composition – this could be PowerPoint, books or prints. Discuss visual focus, what draws the eye into and around a picture, what makes a static or dynamic composition. Use of lines, tone and colour – how this all adds to compositional impact; calm, agitated, balance and imbalance. In sketchbooks, pupils are to draw small images that show a) a tranquil composition and b) an energetic composition, taking elements from the works they have been discussing. Resources include: prints, art books or PowerPoint; sketchbooks, pencils and oil pastels or paints. Create a small table in the back of sketchbooks, classifying the elements of stable and dynamic compositions.	**Homework** Copy either the *Mona Lisa* by da Vinci or *Wham!* By Lichtenstein into sketchbooks and change certain elements to make either the *Mona Lisa* dynamic or *Wham!* Stable.
2–5	Comparing and analysing compositions and considering their purposes and how this is conveyed. Researching and selecting relevant materials and sources. Planning images for a final piece of a modern icon. Production of final, mixed media pieces of modern	Look at images of icons – both contemporary photos and paintings. Discuss what makes an icon? Are religious figures really icons? Are contemporary celebrities really icons? Is hero another word for icon? Discuss with a partner whether the icon is the person, their actions or their image? How does the image enhance a person's appeal? Who makes an icon? Plan a final piece based on a stable or dynamic composition and an icon of your choice. Using a variety of materials and resources, create	Choose an icon from today or the past. Find an image of this person and glue it in your sketchbook. Write an explanation of why you think that person is iconic. Draw a portrait of a family member, using tones and colours to enhance the importance of the image.

icon. Understanding of decorative elements, application of knowledge of composition and skills in the use of mixed media.

a contemporary image of your own icon using appropriate decoration and responses to art you have looked at. Suggested images: Elizabeth I; Krishna; Picasso's *Weeping Woman*; Christ; St George and the dragon; Anubis; Churchill; Buddha; Martin Luther King; Gandhi; Franklin; Klimt's *The Kiss*; any contemporary celebrities. Also required: A3 cartridge paper, paints, glue, scissors, cuttings, prints, collage materials, pencils and sketchbooks.

Find a picture of *the Ambassadors* by Holbein. Note all the personal effects around them, drawing attention to aspects of their lives. In your sketchbook, draw a selection of belongings you think your icon would own, such as a phone; mug; favourite food; item of jewellery or pen. The grouping should be considered – no big gaps between objects and where possible, real objects should be used as reference.

6   Self-assessment/evaluation of work.

Complete work and mount, then fill in self-assessment sheet to evaluate what you have done so far. Paper needed for mounting and pre-prepared self-assessment sheets.

average number of hours a 14–16 year old spends in art lessons is about 75 a year. At A Level students have just over 200 hours of directed time per year – not enough to achieve top results. It has always been accepted that Year 12 and 13 art students need to spend a great deal more time working on their art coursework or exam preparation than is allocated in their timetables. Time restrictions are a constant concern for many art teachers, along with the usual problems of lack of facilities, equipment and storage space. It is therefore helpful, where possible, to provide extracurricular workshops or clubs. As far as lack of resources is concerned, make a list and pin it somewhere prominent or keep it on the department database, asking all members of staff in the department to jot down:

- how often each resource is used
- the year group using it
- how often the resource is used per term
- the project the resource is used for.

In this way, you can work out what materials and equipment are used to a greater or lesser degree.

Planning for GCSE assessment

A chart that explains assessment objectives to your GCSE students is useful so they can check their own progress throughout the course. Here are two examples:

Assessment objective	What this means	% of marks
AO1	Record observations, experiences and ideas in ways that lead you in the directions you have chosen	25
AO2	Analyze and evaluate images, objects and artefacts, showing that you understand any underlying meanings	25
AO3	Develop and explore ideas using a range of media, methods and resources, reviewing and adapting your work as it progresses	25
AO4	Making clued-up connections with the work of others and producing a final piece that meets your aims	25

GCSE Assessment objectives – student sheet

This is a checklist to help you make sure that you cover all the Assessment Objectives for this subject. For each box, be honest with yourself and only tick the boxes if you really mean it! Where you have not ticked any boxes, go back and fill in the gaps in your work

AO1: Record observations, experiences and ideas in ways that meet your aims

Did I:

Collect ideas and resources ☐
Select the information I used ☐
Consider several options ☐
Distinguish between work that appealed to me or was relevant to my work ☐
Record carefully with drawings, paintings and other methods ☐

AO2: Examine your work and the work of others

Did I:

Analyse my own and others' work ☐
Evaluate what worked and what did not work well ☐
Understand ideas behind certain works of art ☐
Consider ideas and methods of other artists ☐
Respond to ideas and methods of other artists ☐

AO3: Develop and explore ideas, using media and resources and use your ability to review, modify and refine your work

Did I:

Develop my ideas ☐
Explore new techniques ☐
Review and modify my work as I progressed ☐
Refine and change things to improve my work ☐

AO4: Make connections with the work of others and produce a personal, informed and thoughtful final piece (N.B. Don't leave making connections until the end – it must be ongoing).

Did I:

Produce a personal response ☐
Make informed connections with the work of other artists ☐
Use my time well ☐

Planning for A level assessment

With A level art, it is no longer enough to simply 'like art.' Students must be committed enough to work extra hours and to push ideas much further than they have done lower down the school. Whatever endorsements you specialize in, students take two or three units at AS level and a further two or three units at A2 level. Each unit should be a journey from a starting point to a realization.

◆ AS units

Choosing the AS coursework unit will probably be a joint effort within the department. From that starting point, you will encourage your students to build a collection of work that shows exploration, research, technique and skill. There are many ways of doing this. You might ask students to produce a work journal or sketchbook and follow this by exploring a theme. You may encourage them to accumulate work following one path within the theme or topic, or you may insist that they develop just one idea. Whatever path you follow, they must relate their work to the ideas and images of relevant artists or designers (not too many; depth is better than breadth) to broaden the context of their work.

The controlled assignment is usually a five or eight hour timed test. You can give your students the paper in February (or about four weeks before they take the exam). This will give them time to plan, prepare and produce a body of work. Once you receive the paper, you should plan how you will introduce and prepare your students for the topic. Successful methods of doing this include a huge sheet on the wall displaying images and words that connect with the theme and suggest ideas, a PowerPoint presentation that suggests ideas and routes, or a booklet with suggestions and ideas.

◆ A2 units

These units are at a higher level than AS units and this should be reflected in the amount and quality of work your students produce. Most exam boards ask students to produce a unit of practical coursework alongside a linked personal study. Finally, their controlled assignment is either a 12 or 15 hour timed test. Again, plan and prepare some guidance for your students and give them the paper as the exam board specifies; usually about four school weeks before they take the exam. One of the differences between AS and A2 is that in A2 students choose their own theme, which should have some personal significance. Their topic should develop as they proceed and they should explain and illustrate these developments as they occur. Remind them that the work they undertake at A2 should show greater maturity than the work they produced at AS. The personal study they produce must relate to the endorsement they are taking. It could relate to a relevant medium, artist, genre, style or history of something they have been exploring. Most personal studies are required to be between 1,000 and 3,000 words. It must show that they have had access to primary sources and must be unique to each student. For this reason, you will need to prepare as each of your students selects his or her topic or theme. Always bear in mind that art at AS and A2 level intends to promote:

- intellectual, imaginative, creative and intuitive powers
- investigative, analytical, experimental, practical, technical and expressive skills, aesthetic understanding and critical judgement
- an understanding of the interrelationships between art, craft and design, and an awareness of the contexts in which they operate;
- knowledge and understanding of art, craft and design in contemporary society and in other times and cultures.

Encouraging student enthusiasm

Students should be made to feel a part of the art department and proud of their achievements. When they see their work on display, whether this is in the art rooms, in corridors or in other places around the school, they feel a sense of pride. For this reason – and to show others in the school what a vibrant and successful department you are – establish regularly changing displays in the art rooms and around the school. This can be rather time consuming, so ask students to get involved. Invite any who would like to come back at lunchtime or after school and show them how to mount 2D artwork on coloured paper or card – equidistant around the two sides and top and slightly deeper at the bottom. Tell them to print labels (displaying name, form, title of project). Even if the work is not the best, include some of the less able students' work and put the best work in the centre of the display.

Either ask verbally or give out short questionnaires at the end of the year to determine which projects worked and which didn't. What did students find disagreeable and why? You won't act on every comment, but if a general consensus emerges about one or more projects, rethink the SoW or programme of study for the following year.

A reward scheme, whereby you select a pupil who worked especially hard during the last lesson has worked well in many schools. Rewards range from a name on the board, to a certificate, to a merit mark (or equivalent) to the wearing of a special badge or hat for one lesson. (You might be surprised at the success and popularity of the latter!) All have been extremely positive and eventually everyone in the class aspires to achieve the 'artist of the lesson award'. Alternatively, you could select four 'artists of the month'. Take their photos (with their consent) and display these either in or near the art rooms or on the school website. Certificates or some form of prize could be given or if it is displayed on the website, an image of the work should be shown for the rest of the academic year. Anyone achieving 'artist of the month' more than twice during the year could be awarded a prize at the end of the summer term.

Practical projects and lesson plans

Ideally, schemes of work (SoW) should build on students' prior learning and expand upon their skills and proficiency in using different materials. All lessons must address all or most of the attainment targets in the National Curriculum. In their experimentation during lessons, students learn not only to handle different materials, but also how to become more adept at analyzing the world around them.

Exploring drawing materials and techniques

The importance of teaching drawing has been mentioned a couple of times already, but it is important! Those who are able to record the appearance of things have highly developed observational skills and can collect a large body of information through their explorations. In general for Key Stage (KS) 3 art lessons, students should be encouraged to experiment with a range of soft and harder pencils as well as charcoal, pastels and graphite sticks. Inks, coloured pencils and felt tip pens should be experimented with as these also allow for different techniques and help dexterity.

Never just tell students to try out the materials – always give them a specific task to support their experimentation. For example, Year 7 pupils could make a chart of marks, pressing firmly or softly; working gently or vigorously; layering; stippling; swirling; hatching and cross-hatching or lifting out with erasers. Remind students not to smudge any medium with their fingers; only pastel should be smudged with paper towel or an artist's *torchon*. They can either have something to draw from, such as a piece of bark, shells or the interiors of fruits or vegetables, or they

Modroc relief of a dress taken from direct observational drawings. Westcliff High School for Girls, Westcliff-on-Sea, Essex

can make a regular chart, commenting in notes how they created each mark.

'Looking through' is an eternally popular project or one-off lesson that encourages pupils to observe and draw carefully. Give students a variety of still life objects from which to choose – these can be manmade or natural – and tell them to draw a large part of their object as if they are looking at it through a window, glass of water, railings or a magnifying glass. Collect old wallpaper or fabric books and give each pupil a sample. They are to reproduce a section of their sample, using whichever materials you have available. Similarly, get them to collect leaves or vegetables and make detailed drawings of them in pencil, pastel and water-colour. They could cut up the vegetables and make clay versions of them once they have explored 2D representations or make prints from their leaf drawings (lino, mono, batik or screen, depending on your preference). In these exercises, they will not only learn to analyze visually, but they will also begin to understand the structures of things, ways in which light plays on objects and about how textures and patterns alter depending on the angles from which we view them.

◆ *Extending experimentation*

After you are confident that your Year 7 pupils can handle dry media competently, allow them access to wet media. Most will have used paint in their previous schools but their experiences will be quite varied. It need not be dull or monotonous, but a certain amount of academic understanding about colour mixing will be beneficial to their work in the long run. Gouache, poster or powder paints are the most straightforward for students to begin with in KS3, although occasionally watercolour, inks and felt tips can be used as well to show differences in mixing and in transparencies. Acrylics are often best left until GCSE, when students are more dexterous and accomplished, while oils are usually left until A level.

Paint application

You should have two of each of the primaries in paint. That is, warm and cool versions of each. You do not need any pre-prepared secondary or tertiary colours, but it is imperative to have white and useful to have black as well. Show pupils how not every red and blue, for instance, produces violet.

A project that introduces colour mixing to students begins with you showing them images by Wayne Thiebaud of cakes and sweets. Provide them with actual cakes, biscuits and sweets to draw enlarged on their paper. They should consider composition, including overlap and negative space and they should use separate paper to try out colour combinations to produce the required ranges of colours needed to complete their Thiebaud-style images.

This will help them to discover how to make appropriate colours, but you also need to help them to learn how to create more translucent and opaque colours. If you are lucky enough to live near to any water – sea, rivers, lakes or even a pond – and you can manage a trip, studying these natural areas can produce extremely exciting depictions, using paint in different thicknesses and hues. 'Under the water' works well in general as an exploratory project and can be developed further with several different activities.

Lesson planning sheet YEAR 7

Timing	Teacher activities and resources	Pupil learning/activities/responses
10 minutes	**Starter:** Sheets displaying different lettering styles on each table. In groups, pupils are to discuss which letters they like best and make a group decision to put the letters in order of preference. Each group should then explain the group's decisions. Questions to ask: How do they choose? What are the main influences on their choices? If the lettering was for a logo of a shop, would their decisions have been different? If it was for a name plate on their bedroom doors, would their decisions have been different? If it was to be inserted into a public building, would their decisions have been different? Discuss.	Looking/considering Group decisions Speaking and discussion Listening
10 minutes	**Introduction:** Show some examples of traditional repeat patterns (e.g. Celtic, Islamic, medieval and Arts & Crafts) and illuminated letter designs. Discuss practical issues about designing and making a 3D illuminated letter based on repeat patterns out of clay. Talk about how other artists have created successful designs. If possible, this could follow-on from a research homework or school trip. Access to resources required, plus sketchbooks, pencils and colouring pencils or water-based paints.	Looking/considering Speaking and discussion Listening
30 minutes	**Main lesson:** Give pupils one or two lessons to gather information to design their illuminated letter, with a view to making it out of clay. Pupils are to make notes – visual and written – about artists' designs they are studying and then they are to begin planning and designing their illuminated letter, taking care to consider the artists' work they have looked at as well as whether they are including figurative or geometric elements, balance of repeat patterning and colour combinations. As they work, the teacher should walk around the class, offering advice and encouragement on an individual basis and sharing guidance collectively. Remind them that their designs are to be interpreted in clay.	Planning and drawing Researching and note taking Listening Looking/considering Technical skills: drawing, colouring/painting, understanding scale and balance
10 minutes	**Plenary:** Question and answer session about planning and designing – problems and achievements encountered and foreseen.	Vocalizing what they have learned and what they should consider Focusing on what to do during the next lesson.

Other materials and methods

Collage, print, 3D and other methods of working are all extremely important parts of secondary education. A selection of project ideas using a variety of materials and methods is provided online. A lesson planning sheet for Year 7 can be found on the previous page.

◆ *Portraits (Year 10)*

Within the group, students take photos of each other using different expressions, lighting effects and unusual angles. Images

Year 10 portraits inspired by Andy Warhol. Westcliff High School for Girls, Westcliff-on-Sea, Essex

are to be downloaded onto computers and then each student is to choose his or her best two shots. Print them in black and white. Next, students are to research the portraits of Chuck Close and Andy Warhol. They are to make notes on the use of paint or print and what effects they create with their images. They are to reproduce a section of one work by each artist. Next, they are to find two portraits by Close and Warhol and, using whatever materials and scale they choose, reproduce these. Annotate them with explanations about the intentions of the artist(s) and what they are about. They are to reproduce their own two portraits (from the black and white photos) in direct response to the two portraits by Close and Warhol on A1 paper or card. Finally, they should analyze their work in light of what they have learned about Close and Warhol; about the materials they used; and about creating self-portraits.

◆ *The urban environment (AS art, unit 1)*

Unit 1 of AS is divided into two sections. Unit 2 is the externally set examination. Throughout the previous summer (after GCSE) and through the first few weeks of the autumn term, students will explore the formal elements of line, tone, colour, shape, texture, pattern, form and structure using a variety of media and processes.

Holiday work should comprise students exploring line, tone, colour, shape, texture and pattern independently. For each theme they are to fill two to three pages of their sketchbooks if these are A3, or one or two pages if their sketchbooks are A2 or A1. Students are encouraged to make notes about and take photos of any urban areas (such as towns or cities) they visit during the holidays. The first week back at school there will be a group discussion and critique of each other's holiday work.

Students will also find artists who have represented the urban environment, such as Piper, Canaletto, Kandinsky, Klee or de Hoogh. They are to find aspects of the artists' work they find interesting and explore and analyze this. Next, using only line and tone, they are to create an image of a town or city that they visited in the holidays. They should do this on A1 paper using charcoal or graphite sticks. Homework should be using line only to draw an image from a window in their home. For this they can use any medium: suggest ballpoint pen, fineliner or pen and ink.

During their next fortnight of lessons, they are to explore the urban environment in terms of colour, shape and texture through screen prints and sponging, rubbing or creating other textured surfaces with collage, wax, Modroc, sand, tissue paper, straw or plaster. Homework should include researching one of the above artists to investigate how he or she uses colour, shape and texture to represent aspects of the urban environment. They are to reproduce aspects of these elements and evaluate the work.

Further lessons include photocopying or scanning their line drawings, enlarging areas and working on the enlarged portions to build up (i) colour, (ii) texture and (iii) shape inspired by their chosen artist. They should work on their photocopies or scans, producing a variety of responses that explore one or two of the elements: line, tone, texture, shape or colour.

During the fifth week of term, they are to explore form, structure and pattern constructing either a relief or a collage, simplifying buildings' form and structure. They should research two further artists who have based their work on these elements, such as any of the Constructivists, Moholy Nagy, Nicholson, Mondrian, Delaunay, Caro or van Doesburg. As usual, they should analyze what they find interesting about the work, the aims of the artists and how they focused on the elements of structure and form. At this point, you might find it useful to visit a gallery or nearby city (or both) and encourage students to begin to concentrate on a particular area of interest. It might be architectural details from buildings, roads, shops, parks or other surroundings; one or more of the formal elements; the effect of media on the urban landscape; how towns are encroaching on the countryside; maps/cartography; the future of the urban environment; local vicinities; or human use of the urban environment.

By week six, you should gather the whole group together and show and discuss what has been produced. What have they discovered? What can they learn from each other's experiences and opinions? They should be encouraged to constructively critique each other's work and make suggestions for individuals' directions and possibilities for further research. They should now begin to develop their ideas independently and outcomes will broaden. Remind them that their investigations must be sustained – they can change their minds and move in a different direction but they will have to explain why they have done this. They are allowed to make 'imaginative leaps', but on the whole their work should show links and connections, i.e. how they travel on their 'journeys'.

◆ *Further ideas emerging from National Curriculum requirements*

The following suggestions for lesson starting points build on National Curriculum requirements. Emphasize the need for careful planning and insist that for any lesson, no pupil rushes headlong into an idea before considering and preparing properly:

- Reflect on and evaluate your own and others' work and negotiate and express shared opinions about it (*e.g. with a partner, design and create a poster describing an icon – featuring in images, the icon's characteristics and qualities*).
- Select, organize and present a range of visual and other information including using a sketchbook. Then reflect on, evaluate and express opinions about how to adapt this (*e.g. in sketchbooks, draw a range of different natural objects and then select one to draw again in a different way, using different media*).
- Study, research and produce an individually designed response (*e.g. respond to a given brief about painting portraits based on Pop Art*).
- Investigate, select, combine and manipulate media, showing increasing independence in how ideas are developed in their own work (*e.g. explore some of the ways in which artists have exploited or rendered the passing of time and using a range of media, create your own interpretation of this*).
- Distinguish and explore codes and conventions in a range of genres, processes and styles (*e.g. use ICT to work out the possibilities of creating an installation made of entirely unexpected materials, reflecting the concept 'growth'*).
- Show independence and imagination in how ideas may be developed in your own work (*e.g. design and make a kinetic work of art*).
- Initiate your own research and then present outcomes of your own investigations in responding creatively to new possibilities (*e.g. create a piece of environmental art as a response to specific requirements*).
- Work collaboratively to identify, discuss and resolve a complex problem with no pre-determined outcome (*e.g. in a group, produce a joint mural or sculpture to that responds to the theme 'speed'*).

Strategies to deliver lessons 5

Every child matters – and in art and design you can achieve this through your approach, encouragement and lesson structure. Throughout secondary school, young people develop rapidly. Art lessons, where they learn to express themselves and explore their perceptions of themselves, others and the world around them, is extremely valuable. Art lessons that go beyond simply learning technical skills and help to develop enthusiasm, ideas and confidence are invaluable to students' holistic development.

Creative and analytical thinking

National Curriculum levels and exam assessment objectives present a structure for your lesson strategies whereby you can create a useful experience for all your students and a good foundation for those who wish to pursue art further. From their first lessons with you, let your students know that your art lessons are going to be enjoyable and fulfilling, but there's a difference between enjoying learning and just having fun. To benefit from their learning experience, they have to pay attention, focus and work hard. This needs to be established from the start. Reiterate your expectations as often as you think needed and tell your students that you will treat them with respect as long as it's reciprocated. Explain that there are two branches of thinking – creative and analytical – and in order to succeed in art they need to be skilled in both. The two types of thinking are not opposites, but they constantly overlap. For instance, you need to think creatively to solve problems and you need to think analytically to decide which creative solution will be best.

CREATIVE THINKING
- thinking of new ideas and ways of working
- seeing a new pattern or connection between something that was not apparent at first

ANALYTICAL THINKING
- working out a problem logically
- testing ideas objectively and seeing the whole picture rationally
- seeing beyond the obvious, judging and detecting bias

◆ *Creating a thinking culture*

Creating a classroom with a strong thinking culture encourages students to develop positive attitudes and skills. It takes a bit of practice and you need to build it into your lessons. Tell your students that we can all learn to think more intelligently. Here are two simple suggestions that will help:

1. Use key vocabulary throughout your lessons. This will enrich students' understanding and language skills, which all helps to augment their creativity.
2. Explain from the start that they will be encouraged to think throughout their art lessons, so they need to be alert from the moment they step into the room.

There are many ways in which art lessons can nurture thinking skills. Simple approaches include not always feeding answers back to students, no matter how tempting this may be. If a student asks your advice about some practical work, be careful not to immediately blurt out your response. Instead, like a counsellor, put the question back to the student and ask what he or she thinks should be done. This is often quite difficult to do – after all, you know what should be done! But if you occasionally hold back and show restraint, you will help your students *think*. Reassure them that the best way to learn is from their own efforts. Teachers often feel ineffectual when they don't give a wise answer or solution for every question, but remember that you are doing the best job of all by empowering your students. Here are further effective methods of encouraging creative thinking:

- fostering an atmosphere where risk taking is seen as productive
- challenging learners to work in different ways
- putting students in groups to motivate each other
- enjoying the work being undertaken
- if students are not good at concentrating for long, introduce short tasks
- include a range of abilities within working groups

◆ *Questioning*

Artistic development can enhance thinking in many ways. Creative thinking skills, such as hypothesis, reasoning, enquiry and evaluation are part of all secondary art lessons and responding to their own and other artists' work are key factors in KS3, 4 and 5. Many art teachers ask questions throughout all art lessons, but particularly in the starter and plenary. Changing the way in which a question is phrased can make a significant difference to the thought processes pupils need to go through before answering, the language they have to use and the extent to which they expose their understanding. By becoming more effective thinkers, in turn students will become more effective learners and so will be able to take charge of their own learning processes. By thinking critically and creatively, each student will move beyond the role of passive receiver of information and into the role of active participant in their learning.

Having to think beyond the information you give them frequently means that students generate explanations, challenge assumptions, make comparisons or apply fresh ideas to new contexts. The types of questions that art teachers generally ask as part of the process of making should promote thinking skills by encouraging students to consider and contemplate their own ideas and purposes with greater clarity. Whatever students answer, always encourage and respect their responses. It is essential that they feel comfortable and respected by you and their peers when answering questions.

Poor questioning can have an adverse effect – boring or discouraging students – so vary your questioning; ask the whole class at times and groups or individuals at others. Ask questions showing the class that you are interested in their replies. Balance your questioning – ask things they can deduce (e.g. what colour paint could you mix with that to make it brighter?) or things they should know (e.g. how will you create a sense of unity in your composition?) Keep your questions open so that pupils have to consider broad answers. Think about why you are asking questions before deciding what to ask. You should be encouraging them to think, not to guess at answers, so it is often worth asking how a pupil came to their answer, in order to give you some insight into the thinking that occurred. Questions to ask to encourage thinking skills and reflection (also given online) include:

- How do you feel about your piece of work?
- What is its theme?
- Do others understand the same theme, or if not what messages do you expect them to receive when looking at your work?
- Does the work remind you of anything? Why does it remind you of that?

- What did you learn as you created your piece of work?
- What has worked well?
- What would you improve? Why and how?
- What do you see in this artwork?
- What words would you use to describe this artwork?
- How would you describe the lines, shapes, textures and/or colours in this work?
- How would you describe this work to a person who could not see it?
- What differences and similarities can you see in these two works?
- What interests you most about this work of art?
- Which objects in this work seem closer to you? Which objects seem further away?
- What do you think is the most important part of this picture?
- How do you think the artist made this work?
- What questions would you ask the artist about this work if s/he were here?
- What title would you give to this painting?
- What do you think is happening in this painting?
- What do you think this artwork is about?
- What do you think is worth remembering about this artwork?

◆ *Some further ideas*

- Before any type of creative thinking stimulus, check that your pupils understand how it feels to be properly listened to and how it feels when you are not listened to. Before you ask questions or introduce a topic to the class, invite one person to the front to watch and notice who is listening and who isn't.
- Introduce your questions to small groups within the class before putting them to the whole class. This allows students to discuss their thoughts and feel more confident offering responses later in front of the whole class.
- When questioning, don't ask the first person who puts his or her hand up, but wait until less sure pupils are volunteering an answer. In this way, you are showing your pupils that you do not expect them to know an answer, but that they should reflect on the question and formulate a well considered answer. Every time you ask a question, wait for one minute before asking someone to answer. Reassure students that they will always be given thinking time to deliberate over a response, pursue a new line of inquiry or consider an alternative cause, explanation or reason. Waiting for people to answer in this way gives everyone a chance to pause and think.

- Emphasize good listening skills by insisting on eye contact, no interruptions, the next speaker briefly summarizing the last speaker's ideas, and so on.
- Leave time for the plenary, however short the lesson, to reflect on progress that has been made.

Some art departments use the 'thinking circles' model, whereby younger pupils sit in a circle or around tables, thinking of and discussing concepts before they come up with ideas for responses to creative problems. If you try this, you need to make sure that no one in the circle or group puts anyone else down and that everyone participates in some way. The difficulty here is that there are usually one or two individuals who speak more and louder than everyone else, making it easy for the quiet students to become even quieter. The only way this will work is if you give them a time limit and walk around the groups, listening, asking questions and arbitrating. Following this, bring everyone back for a full class discussion and see what ideas they have collectively come up with. You could then create a class mind map from their ideas. Always praise any student if you heard him or her suggesting some good ideas. When introducing a topic, be imaginative with stimuli; things to look at, listen to and question. As you talk about the topic, use language such as assumptions, interpretation, definition, assimilation, analysis and so on that help to prompt their creative thinking. Here is a traditional formula for building creative thinking in your classroom:

1. presentation – of a work of art, topic or other stimulus for enquiry
2. thinking time – private reflection on the stimulus
3. discussion 1 – sharing of thoughts and ideas in pairs or small groups
4. lists, drawings or mind maps – 'churning out ideas'
5. discussion 2 – talk about ideas, ask questions around the class
6. selection – of initial ideas from the lists, mind maps and drawings
7. building – creative and critical thinking about one, two or three of the ideas
8. final thoughts – finalizing reflections and ideas.

Many methods for developing thinking skills work exceptionally well in art teaching and can be adapted or modified to suit individual needs. Techniques and strategies to enhance pupils' thinking skills appear in many of the suggestions throughout this book. The key to teaching thinking is to encourage students to take cognitive action. Here are some tips:

- when making decisions, encourage students to come up with several options
- they should look beyond the obvious when considering a problem
- they should always challenge assumptions and seek unexpected solutions
- they should make connections with ideas and other artists' work
- they should anticipate potential obstacles and consequences in their work
- they should make sketches and mind maps to illustrate their ideas and concepts

Motivating students

Motivation depends on the extent to which teachers are able to satisfy students' needs, to feel in control of their learning, competent and connected with others. So in order to engage pupils from Year 7 onwards, consider what motivates them. You need to appeal to their natural curiosity; their interest in the learning task and the satisfaction they will gain from the lesson's activity.

Personal and expressive work that develops from direct observation and allows students to assess the world and their experiences appeals to students of this age and encourages their development in many ways. Whenever possible, start lessons by asking a question or giving the class a challenge or problem to solve. In this way, you will appeal to their natural curiosity in wanting to find out more or to solve a problem. Allow them to undertake activities that satisfy their investigative and creative needs. This approach will promote an increased understanding of materials and processes. It will enable them to develop their exploratory powers and the ability to communicate verbally and visually. By building new skills and competencies in this way, students develop *intrinsic* motivation; that is, enthusiasm that stems from genuine interest in the problem, practical task and personalized solution. As already discussed, by generating enquiry through questioning and discussion you will help to raise students' achievement.

Once practical work is underway, stimulate further reflection and enthusiasm with more open questioning:

- What would be a wrong material for this work? Why would it be wrong?

- Which other materials could you try using?
- What will you try doing in this work that you have not tried before?
- How could you make your ideas flow better?
- What new skills are you learning with this artwork?
- What parts are the most prominent?
- How could you make everything look flat and without any depth?
- Do you want the work to be realistic, fantastic, expressive, formal, or a mixture of styles?
- What has been the most difficult aspect of creating this work and why?
- What do you need to do next?

◆ *Giving control*

There are ways of letting pupils feel in control of their learning without you losing control of what and how you teach. You still need to consider your own content and objectives, but you can give your pupils a feeling of ownership by discussing decisions and conditions behind the work you set them, so giving them the chance to shape their learning as well as accepting the reasons some aspects of a course are not negotiable.

Wherever possible, allow your students to determine class rules and procedures, set objectives, select learning activities and assignments and decide whether to work in groups or independently. Of course, this is not always practicable so only do this when your programmes of study (PoS) allow it. By providing plenty of material and visual stimuli, you are enriching students' experiences. Collect art books, prints, photographs and posters as well as 'props' – both manmade and natural.

Effective lessons

All pupils need guidance and structure in their lessons, but this does not necessarily mean prescription teaching or an authoritarian teaching style. Art is a subject that lends itself to particularly flexible and inspired teaching – within reason. Art teachers can moderate their lessons to suit the individuals in their lessons. The key component of effective lessons is your knowledge of the subject. The more you understand and know about the topic, the greater skills and knowledge you can impart and the greater respect you will receive from your pupils. In addition to knowing your subject, you should also impart your enthusiasm for the subject and your willingness and ability to explain points clearly and at your pupils' level.

Effective art lessons are often where the teacher establishes his or her authority from the start; he or she organizes each lesson thoroughly and students accept and follow the prearranged plan purposefully and confidently in an atmosphere of mutual respect and understanding. From the other side, students learn best when they are engaged, interested, receptive and focused. It is up to you to develop this approach in all lessons. By maintaining a regular routine and structure, when students enter your art room they will quickly accept how things are done and establish the right frame of mind from the moment they arrive. The following is by no means set in stone, but is a suggestion of a structure that works well.

◆ Suggested lesson structure

Start the lesson quickly. When pupils arrive they should go to their designated seats and wait in silence to be told to sit. All unnecessary equipment should be placed under the tables, leaving work surfaces clear. Registration should be called, with the lesson starter or introduction following immediately. Present the content of the lesson clearly and at pupils' level. This fast-paced start should set the tone for the entire lesson.

Explain the lesson objectives clearly, in terms of what pupils will learn rather than what they will do. Encourage pupil participation and attention at all times. As the main part of the lesson gets underway, introduce key vocabulary. Any important words should be recorded at the back of students' sketchbooks. During the main part of the lesson use strategies that promote pupil understanding and the development of technical skills, such as demonstrations, questioning, listening and discussion. During whole class demonstrations, pupils should be organized around a central work area. Use key vocabulary throughout demonstrations and make sure that pupils are respectful of each other's contributions. Make sure that everyone is clear so they are able to put what you have demonstrated into practice. Move around the room to ensure pupils have the correct equipment and are working correctly. As you do this, assess pupils' understanding, level of practical skill and progress. Some pupils will be able to work without further teacher intervention; others will need more guidance.

Bring the lesson to a close leaving plenty of time to clean and tidy the art room. Conclude the lesson with a plenary, recapturing pupil awareness of the learning that has taken place and deliberately drawing together the planned and chance events of the lesson. Use exemplar work to establish whether or not the objectives have been met.

◆ Key points for effective art lessons

- *Be prepared*: Make sure your planning is thorough and organized and that your lessons are well structured. Practical activities should be prepared for with materials in place and students seated in an appropriate manner.
- *Keep the pace*: Maintain interest and fluidity throughout each lesson, which often means matching tempo to pupils' learning; make sure that you can multitask!
- *Make smooth transitions*: from one activity to another. Don't leave pupils waiting, but maintain the flow of each lesson, no matter what arises.
- *Suitability and clarity*: Make sure that all your explanations suit pupils' abilities. Demonstrate practical activities where necessary. Challenge the class wherever possible, but don't focus so high that they give up.
- *Authority*: Maintain your firmness while developing a good rapport with your pupils. Establish mutual respect from the start.
- *Be alert*: Notice everything. You need to maintain awareness throughout each lesson. Know when pupils' attention is flagging; when anyone misbehaves; or when things are not going as smoothly as they should, and deal with it quickly.
- *Motivate*: Interact and encourage pupils' progress whenever possible. Maintain your enthusiasm and constructive approach to stimulate creativity and diligence.

◆ Mind maps

The theory behind mind mapping is that ideas create more ideas. Most children learn about mind maps, which they often call spider diagrams, thought cascading or brainstorming in primary school. Mind maps are one of the ways in which you can help students to develop their ideas and become enthused. To do this, they should write down every idea they have that is associated with a problem. Tell them that every idea is as valid as the last and they should just keep adding ideas, almost without thinking, filling a page of their sketchbooks. They can produce mind maps individually or in pairs at the start of a topic. There is more about mind mapping in Chapter 7.

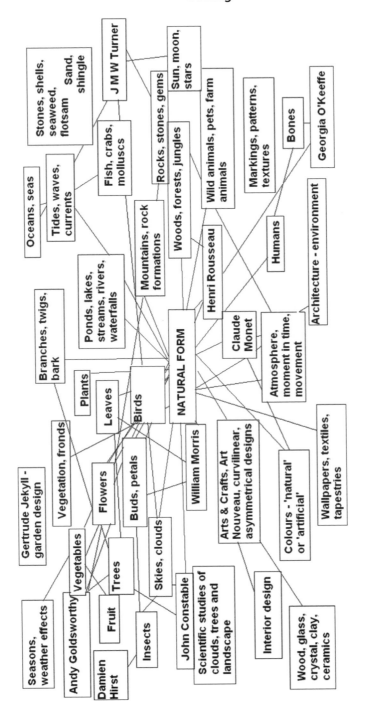

◆ Visiting an art gallery

A vital part of secondary art education is taking students to galleries or museums where they can see art at first hand. Feeling relaxed when being surrounded by and looking at works of art is one of the ways in which you can enrich your students' experience. These visits help them take imaginative leaps with their own work. Although, of course, art is all around us, it is important for young people to see and experience as broad a range of art as possible and at close hand. To see this with you whereby you can explain issues and aspects of the art and answer questions is particularly valuable.

Reproductions are an inferior substitute for real objects – dimensions, colours, textures and surroundings in which works are placed are vital elements to be experienced at first hand. Ideally, the enjoyment of visiting a gallery or museum will encourage students to want to return independently, perhaps soon after the school visit and in years to come. There is more about educational visits in Chapter 10.

◆ PoS to encourage a thoughtful classroom

Most young people are naturally creative. By encouraging and guiding their creativity, you will equip them with the tools to develop in many different ways; not only in art lessons. After the age of 14, if students wish to progress with art they usually study it for GCSE. An example of a plan for the start of a PoS for GCSE art is given online. Encouraging students to contemplate their own ideas and to understand their own purposes, it leads them through a variety of activities and concepts.

Organization

Secondary school art rooms need to be different from other subject classrooms as they are used for both practical and theory learning and work will often be left either in progress or for display. In addition, a vast amount of materials and equipment are needed. Unfortunately, school art rooms are rarely as well equipped as those in art colleges, but there are ways in which you can build on what you have. It often seems that when many secondary schools were built, the architects and administrators were unaware of the requirements and safety considerations for learning visual art and this is frequently a stumbling block, whether the school is old or new. Part of your planning should always take into consideration the room layout, placement of furniture, light and equipment storage.

◆ The art rooms

The art room layout will affect the ways in which you plan and deliver your lessons. An essential requirement is that the environment is visually stimulating, with regularly changing student displays to inspire and enliven imaginations and attitudes. Most art rooms are restricted in some ways, often with limited space, large or cumbersome desks, tables or chairs, inefficient sinks or a lack of light. These impediments are fairly common, as is not being able to access the room before your lesson begins as it is shared space. This latter problem can be eased with portable materials and equipment, sympathetic colleagues (who vacate the room promptly at the end of their lesson) and able bodied students who help to move furniture or hand out work, for instance.

Preparing lessons for poorly equipped or problematic art rooms is challenging and emphasizes the need for careful planning. Your room layout will affect the ways in which pupils interact with each other and you. In the majority of secondary school art rooms, pupils are grouped around tables in groups of between four and six, giving good opportunities for group work. This can also mean that not all students will be facing you and it is easy for them to talk to each other rather than concentrate on what you are saying. This can make your job of managing behaviour more difficult, so be aware of this and either try to change things around (not always possible) or make pupils face you at all times between tasks. Often, it has been noted that 'naughty' children tend to sit on tables nearest the door while better behaved children congregate on tables closer to the teacher. If you find this and it proves unmanageable for you, stick to a designated seating plan.

◆ Demonstrations

There is no better way to teach a technique or method of working than by demonstrating it to your students. By demonstrating a technique proficiently and explaining what you are doing logically and clearly as you work, you should engage everyone in the class. Pupils who have used the technique before will discover new ideas or reinforce old ones while pupils who have never before applied the technique will gain confidence and feel motivated to try it.

If you do not have suitable facilities for demonstrations in your art room, find an area where you can both work and accommodate students. You should have prepared the area before you begin the lesson. Tell students to gather round you. This encourages them to focus on what you are showing them and to ask appropriate questions (more intimate gatherings encourage even the shyest pupils to speak up). Always make sure that no one is lurking at the back, not paying attention or unable to see. People in the front could sit on chairs or stools to give viewers at the back a chance to see.

◆ Display areas

Make sure that you have lots of display space around the room and, if possible, outside the door as well. If you don't already have it, put in a request for a display cabinet for 3D work. Try to keep some display walls clear in the room so a class can put up all their work and discuss it in the plenary. An art class that does not display and discuss their own work is missing out on worthwhile learning. Display spaces around the school also provide a convenient way to share work with other students, teachers and visitors to the school. Displaying work helps to motivate

If lack of display space is an issue, exhibit the work in a random overlapping arrangement, as here. Year 9 'Icons', Westcliff High School for Girls, Westcliff-on-Sea, Essex

students when they see their hard work and achievements recognized in this way. Displays also help to pull the school together and to raise the image and status of the art department.

◆ *Windows and blinds*

Art, probably more than any other subject in the school, needs windows for its sources of light and ventilation, observational drawing and for teaching about space, depth and perspective. Yet there are often occasions when you need to darken the room for presentations and so on. Many art teachers resort to pinning black sugar paper or black plastic bin bags across the windows, but if possible try to obtain dark, opaque blinds or curtains.

◆ *Wet and dry areas*

Ideally there should be enough sinks for a class of 30 to be able to wash up their equipment speedily. They should be large enough for several people to stand by them without congesting the rest of the room. The areas behind them should be tiled and draining space should also be large. Dry areas should ideally be some distance away from the wet areas, but this is not always possible in a school art room. As a compromise, try to keep things separate. Perhaps have a desktop drying rack a short distance away from the sink and shelves to keep completed projects, work in progress and props further away still.

◆ Colours and surfaces

Walls in art rooms should be neutral and washable. The atmosphere needs to be created through the artwork on the walls and around the room, not by the décor. In addition, flat or horizontal surfaces should be materials that are easily washed or wiped down. Table tops and surfaces by sinks should be easily wiped and floors should be able to be washed as often as necessary.

◆ Desks/easels

Always try to furnish art rooms with desks or easels that tilt at an angle. Recent trends in many art rooms have been for flat table tops, which damage pupils' backs and mean they have to bend over their work, so in effect they are working in their own shadows. This arrangement is highly unsatisfactory and should be avoided or changed if at all possible. Not only is it good practice to work at a more vertical angle, but it will prevent many back and neck problems in later life.

If you are stuck with horizontal table tops, see if you can buy table top easels or even foldaway easels that can be used by smaller classes. Alternatively, have drawing boards with special drawing board paper clips. It's not ideal, but this means that students can balance drawing boards, at least when they're drawing, on their laps, tilting them upwards. The best types of tables or desks are those that can be moved by students, from flat to almost upright. This allows for a horizontal working space for 3D work and angled work surfaces for drawing, painting, printing and so on.

◆ Storing materials, equipment and resources

Most art departments need more space for storing students' work, props, materials and equipment, so they must be organized. You and your colleagues need to be firm about returning previous students' work and keeping equipment in its correct place. This could be plan chests or vertical racks against the walls, or, if you're lucky, separate walk-in cupboards. Every art room should have a drying rack or washing line for drying paintings. All secondary art rooms have practically nonstop traffic of different groups of students using the same space. You need to be extremely organized with the way you store your materials, equipment, work in progress and completed projects.

Preferably you will have a walk-in cupboard or store room for your art materials and equipment. This should contain all you need and use for practical work. For your own ease and speed of use, always keep things in the same space. Paper should be laid flat on shelves; pencils, paints, collage materials, brushes, scissors, craft knives, glue and other general equipment should be in their own areas. Clay, Modroc, printing equipment and chemicals, such as white spirit, should be kept in another area. Sketchbooks should have their own place too. This whole area should be out of bounds for all students – it cannot be emphasized enough, for several reasons, why they should not have access to this.

Two areas that students should have access to though are the art books (of which you should have a large and varied collection) and computers, so they can use the internet for research. Art books can be bought cheaply off the internet, from libraries and from discount shops. Keep on the look out! As well as the internet, it's also helpful to put things on the school intranet that will be of use to pupils when they're researching. This can include quick links to art galleries, images and text about various artists and art movements, other useful ideas, resources and exemplar work by previous pupils.

Next, you will probably have files of letters, notes, lesson plans, worksheets, specifications, past and current assessments and various other important documents. The general idea is to reduce these and keep paper documents to a minimum, but nobody seems to have reached this yet – and if you've photocopied worksheets that have been returned, it's a waste to simply put them in the recycling bin when they could be reused with other classes. Most schools are now almost completely computer literate in that teachers write and store their reports, schemes of work (SoW), lesson plans and assessment material on computers.

Most schools use learning platforms and other school information management systems. You can use yours to improve pupil performance, keep records of assessment grades and homework marks so you can track all your pupils' progress speedily and accurately to measure the success of your teaching strategies. You can even manage the examinations process and create individual education plans to ensure that all your pupils, including those with special educational needs, are supported with skilful target setting. Using the system you can write reports at school or home and transfer one to the other. You can store letters sent out to parents and plan your lessons and homework.

Even if you are not computer literate, it is worth getting used to methods of inputting information into documents on the computer and saving them there as this keeps paperwork to a minimum and will save you time in the long run. If you still prefer keeping your own books or folders of these things, it's best to keep these in addition to saved files on the computer.

◆ *A summary of considerations for art room organization*

- Even if students have to sit around tables so their backs are towards you as they work, make it a rule from the start of the year that when you are speaking, they turn round and you can see everyone's eyes.
- Ensure enough space for each pupil to work without having to hold in their elbows or pile their bags or blazers on top of each other's.
- Have a drying rack in each art room or, less practical but better than nothing, a washing line where paintings can be left to dry.
- Have a desk on which to place your lesson plan, laptop and other equipment you might need. Make sure that your pupils know they may not touch anything on or in your desk without your specific permission.
- Storage for students' work – suggestions: A1 folders for each KS3 class and individually after that; drawers, shelf or cupboard space for each class or group.
- More than one large sink per art room with enough space around them so that more than one student can stand at them at any one time.
- Large windows with working blinds.
- Interactive whiteboard.
- Area for teacher demonstrations.
- Enough space around tables to allow for speedy evacuation of the room if necessary.

Of course, most of this is out of your hands, but these are the basic requirements of any art department and the senior management team should work with you on this if your rooms are not quite there yet.

◆ Cleaning up

Another part of your organization should include the time it takes each class to clear away. It is important that you teach everyone, from the start, to be responsible for their own mess. For younger classes, you can organize monitors to undertake selected tasks or make them clear up table by table. If you opt for monitors, you must change them each term or half term or the whole class will leave the tasks to the few students who always want to help. If you take the table by table option, there is going to be a point when a number of pupils are sitting round their tables, waiting. Alternatively they should all form a queue and wash what they have used. You might consider posting a pupil by each sink to ensure that everyone is washing up their own things and not simply leaving them in the sink. If you do this, you might also need to post a couple of pupils to assist in putting work away or wherever it is going at the end of the lesson.

A cleaning chart is always useful to let everyone know what is expected of them. This should include not only washing up and putting away any equipment they have used and the work they have produced, but also wiping down tables and chairs; cleaning round the sink; picking up scraps off the floor; putting away any unused materials; and tidying any equipment drawers or cupboards.

◆ Computers and whiteboards

Ideally, your computer should be on and ready at the start of each lesson. As well as registers and your own planning and diary, it is a good idea to keep all your resources in electronic files if you can. Storing your resources, SoW and lesson plans on the computer saves time and storage space. Backing all this up on a memory stick is sensible and means you can choose whether to work on these at school or at home. Create subfolders for different year groups and topics and put useful resources and hyperlinks on the school intranet. Let students know they are there and encourage students to use them. Whether your department or the ICT technician creates the art section on the intranet, make sure that it is divided into manageable and easily recognized areas, such as KS3, GCSE and A level, with relevant material in each. Whiteboards, ordinary or interactive, are useful in a number of ways:

- if you are showing images, as you can draw on them to demonstrate a point

- questions, topics, suggestions and ideas can be listed on them
- mind maps can be semi-drawn, leaving students to continue and build on your starting points
- step by step progress of a technique or building up of a subject can be shown
- examples of students' work can be demonstrated and others can critique this
- students can adjust images and demonstrate their knowledge with them
- if you involve your students with the material on the board, they will remain active participants in your lesson, rather than passive, bored viewers

Improving the quality of the learning environment

By making the arts a visible and integral part of school life, the art learning experience can be greatly improved. Artwork displayed around the school also improves the quality of the physical environment. It makes a huge difference to visitors' experiences and impressions of a school where artwork is displayed prominently, making the whole environment exciting and stimulating. Similarly, art events such as exhibitions, can create a sense of unity within the school; can give older pupils a chance to act as role models; and are an exciting way to introduce pupils to a new KS. Trips to art galleries or museums and opportunities to work with artists in the school, helps to broaden pupils' experiences. Some schools make the arts more visible by having artists in residence over a term or a year.

The arts generate significant energy and excitement.

◆ *Display and exhibitions*

Display can be used for many purposes, such as: raising the profile of the art department; assisting teaching through evaluation of pupils' work in progress and on completion; raising pupils' esteem; encouraging them to produce further high quality work; demonstrating techniques, processes and approaches; communicating information, such as assessment objectives or end of KS3 levels; illustrating influences of other artists' and designers' work; or displaying GCSE and A level work for the moderators to come and assess in June. Similarly, the opportunity to exhibit pupils' work either in school, in the local community or further afield, is one of the most significant opportunities that art teachers have to raise the profile of the subject. Exhibitions of pupils' work can often be of great inspiration to those pupils whose work is on display and others in their class. Exhibitions of KS4 or 5 work inspire younger pupils to want to reach the same standard, to take the subject at GCSE or A level and to try out materials and methods as seen in the exhibition.

It is worth taking time to plan a private view for other teachers, parents and friends of the exhibitors, school governors and colleagues from higher education establishments. If possible, provide refreshments and musical accompaniment. Ideally, you could involve the food technology and music departments. Advertise the event and invite the local press – ask (sensible) students if they'll agree to be interviewed and photographed. (Most will love this and will be proud to talk about their work.) If you do not have the facilities in your school, consider other venues such as the local library, town hall, theatre or even local shopping mall, but be aware that these things usually need to be booked about 18 months in advance. Once you have established the exhibition, if you want to make it an annual event, it will be easier to put it in place after the initial occasion.

When displaying work, pupils should be shown how to trim paper with a trimmer, to mount work (evenly at the top and two sides and slightly deeper along the bottom edge) and to fix paper on to mounting paper/board with a small dab of glue in each corner, staples, dressmaker pins or drawing pins – all put in neatly and used minimally. They should display a variety of work, showing different techniques, media and subjects and should differentiate between preparatory work and final pieces. Mounted work should be clearly labelled – all details should be apparent for the moderator – and any decoration should be either nonexistent or minimal, unless it is part of the work. Two-dimensional work should be displayed aligning horizontals and verticals, not haphazard or angled in any way. Some overlap might create an interesting, busy display, but not too much or it could create confusion. Tell students to imagine their work is on a grid, with gaps or spaces in between in straight lines. These spaces can be varied but all lines (edges of works) should be parallel to each other. Three-dimensional work or works on computers need to be set up near to any 2D displays.

Sketchbooks and work journals

7

Picasso once said, '...I picked up my sketchbooks daily, saying to myself, "What will I learn of myself that I didn't know?"'

From their first art lessons at secondary school, all pupils should be encouraged to keep a work journal or sketchbook and take ownership of their work. The act of keeping a sketchbook and the process by which students do this is extremely important on many levels and so should be introduced as early in their art education as possible.

Thinking around problems

If they have become accustomed to recording notes, ideas and techniques and in making their sketchbooks unique and personal to them during Key Stage (KS) 3, students will be proficient at this by the time they reach GCSE and A level. Even if students do not continue studying art beyond the age of 14, the creation of sketchbooks will have helped them to develop creative and visual thinking skills. Sketchbook techniques constitute some of the main strategies for developing thinking skills, including mind mapping, questioning and enquiring, thinking around a problem, seeking unusual solutions, sketching, analyzing and investigating.

Traditionally used by artists, sketchbooks are the best way for artists to develop and consolidate their ideas and can be formed in a multitude of ways. Whatever the method and approach, sketchbooks are an essential and effective means by which to inspire and stimulate students. After KS3, sketchbooks make up a large part of pupils' preparation studies for their art GCSEs and A levels. Because all the assessment objectives have to be met

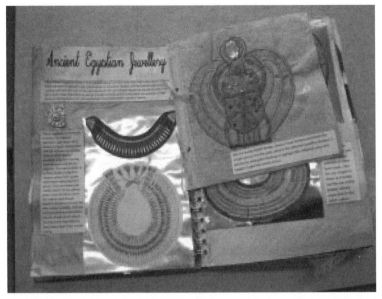

Making creative use of a sketchbook using a variety of materials and exploring ancient cultures. Loreto College, St Alban's, Hertfordshire

within the preparation, and often most of this is completed in sketchbooks, in terms of marks sketchbooks have more weighting than final pieces.

Visual enquiries

When you first give pupils of 11 their own sketchbooks, you might wonder how they will ever develop that enquiring, exploratory approach that hopefully develops by the time they take art at GCSE. It is, however, worth persevering! At 11 years old most children see all school books as similar entities – to be treated in the same way. They do as you ask, but just that, no more and no less. There is rarely any original or investigative work undertaken. Alternatively, if you ask them to use their sketchbooks for examining the world around them and their creative skills, filling pages with ideas and visual enquiries, you might find that they waste pages, using the books rather like a rough book, full of unproductive doodles or cartoons and often simply drawing one small image on a page. So a balance needs to be met.

From the start, tell pupils that you will be setting work to be completed in their sketchbooks and they should use each page fully, but in between set work they can explore ideas independently, albeit related to their current art project. Reward those pupils who make efforts beyond the set work; those who research and investigate ideas and information that help them to develop their class work further and to think in a broader way about the topic.

Helping students achieve their potential

Explain that although you expect their books to be as interesting, bold and complex as they can manage, students should not be too precious about their work – mistakes are allowed and should be left. Girls in particular often try to create pristine sketchbooks and if they feel their work is not good enough, frequently either stick pages together or tear pages out. This is to be discouraged! The more they use their sketchbooks, the more their confidence will develop and so they will improve and create the kind of books you are endorsing.

Sketchbooks rarely contain final pieces of work. They are personal records of students' interests, embellished according to their tastes and annotated according to their understandings. Tell your students that their sketchbooks are for class and homework, but they are also to be their individual creations; each book is to be a journey of discovery in which they develop personal style, ideas and skills and gain insights into areas that you will be exploring in art lessons. By reminding students to use their sketchbooks frequently, you will encourage them to become visual thinkers. They should use their sketchbooks to record and work out ideas, gather information and respond to things around them. Sketchbooks are also places to experiment with media that they are not familiar with. You need to get the balance right with assisting students here. The books should be personal to them, but they should also be shared with you and others in their class. They need to select and decide on the content, but you need to make suggestions to help them achieve their potential.

◆ *The sketchbook as a journey*

Sketchbooks can be used for many purposes, including: gaining insights and ideas; to document and record information and

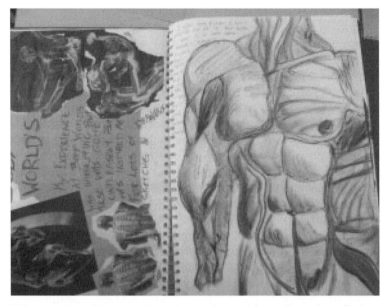

Using a variety of images, viewpoints and materials, students do well when they explore things that interest them. King Edmund School, Rochford, Essex

experiences; to observe the world; to remind yourself of experiences and discoveries; to initiate further ideas for future projects; and to encourage creativity and imagination. Emphasize the importance of everyone making his or her own sketchbook individual and different from each other's, full of personal thoughts and artistic developments. Mention the well-known sentiment that every sketchbook is a journey and not a destination. Tell them that they can decorate some pages, but there also needs to be space for written notes, visual explorations, drawings and paintings. When you set sketchbook work, whole pages should be used for large drawings, paintings and written notes. Make it clear to pupils from their first art lessons that sketchbooks may contain:

- quick drawings, sketches and visual notes
- interesting objects that they have found, e.g. leaves, tickets, wrappers, fabric
- careful observational drawings and paintings
- photographs
- design developments, mind maps, thumbnail sketches
- records of gallery, museum or exhibition visits

- key vocabulary
- written notes
- class and homework assignments.

Sketchbooks should be pupils' unique books in which they explore, research and develop creative ideas related to their art lessons. There are no real rules for or set methods of working in them, although you need to support and guide your students. Encourage risk taking and experimentation and try to discourage restricted or unadventurous work. Show them how to continue and expand on their investigations and how to fill each page to create interesting and distinctive studies. One of the primary functions of art in secondary school is to give students the opportunities and skills to respond visually to their personal experiences. By using their sketchbooks regularly, they will develop greater confidence in their own capabilities and abilities to explore and respond to their individual perspectives. As a part of this, they will gain a feeling of responsibility and ownership, which will fuel pride and determination to do well. Remind them of what you expect them to achieve in their sketchbooks:

- fluency of thought and understanding
- development of ideas and imagination
- identification of problems and possibilities
- resolution of visual problems
- expansion of artistic vocabulary
- inspiration and stimulation of ideas
- making associations and connections with the work of others

Moving on

At GCSE and A level, sketchbooks become especially important, as preparation work is worth approximately 75 per cent of the overall mark. Students must follow the assessment criteria, but the most successful sketchbooks demonstrate nonconformity and fluency through a variety of working methods, including a body of drawings and paintings from direct observation and investigations that assist their development of insight, understanding and knowledge. Work should be unselfconscious and uninhibited. Encourage students to move away from narrow, linear development towards more freely expressive practice, while making sure that they meet the criteria.

Year 9 perspective work (King Edmund School, Rochford)

The assessment objectives are set to encourage just that sort of approach. Students should use their work journals to observe, record and store information; to research and collect; to express themselves and stretch their imaginations; to invent and design; to experiment with ideas and materials; to investigate and analyze the work of other artists and to develop different ways of seeing and depicting. These are all part of the coursework and preparation for the timed tests at GCSE and A level. Preparation studies support each unit of work and should meet all of the assessment objectives, which are roughly:

- *AO1*: Create drawings, paintings, 3D responses, photos and so on connected with the theme. These should be based on primary sources.
- *AO2*: Analyze and respond to other artists and designers' methods of dealing with similar subjects and themes.
- *AO3*: Experimentation with different methods and materials.
- *AO4*: The final piece, which brings together ideas from the whole unit.

◆ *Practical matters*

Sketchbooks or work journals can be any size or format and students should produce several over the GCSE and A level periods. Some schools find that working on sheets of A1 or A2 and then binding everything together at the end of each unit creates the most inspired work journal, giving students a sense of freedom for experimentation, while other schools let students choose and use a variety of shop bought sketchbooks throughout the course. One thing – if students want to use small A5 sketchbooks, this will not usually suffice and should be supplementary to larger books. They are fine for making visual notes and jottings, but will not be sufficiently large enough to include and show details required to meet the assessment objectives.

Whether you supply the sketchbooks or students buy their own, insist on good quality paper or they will have to constantly glue in pieces of thicker, better quality paper. Having said that, some students manage well with black paper pages or thin brown, parcel paper pages. In general, thick cartridge paper, A3 sketchbooks work well as they accommodate and withstand a large variety of materials and techniques, while students can include larger pieces either separately or folded in the pages. Thick cartridge paper can withstand a variety of punishing treatments.

Similarly, A level sketchbooks or work journals should be large enough to show development and exploration and there should be several bulging sketchbooks by the end of the course. It is easy to say that it is quality that counts, not quantity, and of course this is true – to a certain extent. If there is not enough work, there will simply not be sufficient quality to gain the top grades. Tell students to bear in mind that they should use their work journals to develop ideas and practical work; experiment with theories, materials and techniques; record images and observations; and present their findings visually and in written notes.

◆ *Research and experimentation*

Although some students have recently been experimenting with electronic or 'virtual' sketchbooks, most exam boards and professional practices prefer hard copy sketchbooks, even if these are in addition to electronic sketchbooks. Students can include, along with traditional materials, scanned or digital images. However they work, you must encourage students to research, experiment and explore ideas and materials. They should develop their ideas in whichever ways suit them – drawing from direct observation, secondary sources, memory or imagination; collecting images and altering or manipulating them; collage; painting; printmaking; writing or drawing diagrams and so on – using as wide a variety of media as they can. Sketchbooks should be with students at school, at home, in art galleries, on holiday and anywhere else they can take them. The books should become their personal visual diaries – records of their observations, thoughts and feelings, containing in-formation that is unique to their own experiences and view-points.

Guide your students as much as you can, while allowing them the freedom to move in their own directions. Introduce them to methods of preparing or building up their ideas by investigating the problem, gathering relevant data and planning what they will do next. Here is where mind maps and lists work well, as does researching in books and on the internet (as long as it's focused). Tell them to concentrate firmly on the problem and to keep thinking, researching and planning in this way, almost until they feel saturated with the problem. Then they should stop thinking about it. Just that; move away from their thoughts and allow the natural processes of the mind bring ideas forth. They will find that all their prior focus and deliberation will make ideas assimilate in their subconscious minds and fresh ideas will come to the fore. Once again, they should use their sketchbooks and churn out as many thoughts and concepts as they can. Finally, they should work compre-hensively through their ideas.

There is no one particular way of using a sketchbook, although the majority of students will use a book full of sheets of good quality paper as discussed above. Encourage students to personalize their sketchbooks, using collage, cut outs, pop-ups, found materials, textiles and anything else that creates a tactile, individual object that contains their thoughts, research and observations that lead on to separate, more finished pieces. A word of warning – take care that students do not work for too long on decorating pages. This may sound obvious, but there have been trends whereby some students spend an inordinate amount of time personalizing their journals at the expense of content. Examiners are not impressed by beautiful pages that feature little consequential content.

◆ *Progression*

Although students must be encouraged to show progression and development throughout their work journals, when it comes to marking work has to be separated into certain areas for assessment. So in their work journals, students must produce clear evidence that they have met each of the criteria, which include observational recording skills, responses to primary sources, investigations, analyses and critical and contextual understanding of the work of other artists and cultures. Originally a way of eliminating subjective marking by examiners, this method ensures that all candidates are marked at an equal level to the same criteria.

Although this method makes assessment impartial, it also means that it is now possible for students with poor creative and technical abilities to attain a decent grade, while some particularly creative students can be marked down if there is insufficient evidence of any of the assessment objectives. This follows that it is essential for students to show that they are meeting or exceeding the assessment objectives in their work journals.

For some years, many art teachers have criticized these assessment methods, particularly the insistence that students respond critically to the work of other artists. Critics claim that this can be an obstacle if students are producing exciting work and have to stop to consider different cultures, themes and thoughts of other artists or designers. Yet this needn't be the case. If you train your students to think about other artists' work or methods while they are creating their own practical responses and to jot down thoughts and feelings in between creative work, they will soon produce enough written work to meet the required assessment criteria. The plan is to get them to think in

Using the entire page of a work journal at GCSE to express emotion. King Edmund School, Rochford, Essex

the right way and to write down those thoughts without worrying about it. Be aware too that although detailed documentation will show how they reached their ideas and can help to broaden the work they are doing, there are ways of doing this without having to write extensively.

Resources and reflections

From their first lessons with you, encourage your students to look at the work of other artists. This is where your subject knowledge needs to be sharp (or you should at least know where to tell them to look)! You need to be able to suggest artists, craftspeople or designers to suit each student and to inspire them with fresh ideas. Although of course your knowledge will not be limitless, you will inevitably often recommend your favourites, but try not to become repetitive! A good resource base is invaluable and students will often enjoy looking through books and other resources, either with you or with their peers, weighing up which artists or designers might be pertinent to their own work. Ideas can come from many sources, including drawings of what they see around them, clippings from magazines, photocopies from books, postcards, photographs, images downloaded from websites, samples of textures, fabrics and other materials.

As places to gather information about and comment on how things look, how they are made and how they work, part of the process is learning to write information or comments about what is in an image. These comments should be students' own personal reactions. Many students find that reflective writing helps them to consider their intentions and address issues more deeply. Whether they write a little or a lot, help individuals to choose words that emphasize important details. They should write down their ideas using key vocabulary to help the moderators understand what they are thinking, but they can illustrate their thoughts as well. Two pictures with short, simple captions can often show a clear comparison of ideas without many words. Apart from writing, printed images, drawings and doodles responding to different aspects of original work often explain the underlying thinking in many cases, showing that the student has investigated a range of ideas and methods and has used these as building blocks for his or her own work. Students can show ideas and influences by jotting down thoughts and details of artists' work in bullet points; circling, highlighting or underlining words from printed information; typing notes (on a variety of papers) or showing comparative ideas, so they are demonstrating visually what and how they are analyzing, such as an exploration of many different types of texture or pattern.

Whatever they do, students must show that they have evaluated and analyzed other artists' work through their own art. This can be done at GCSE without a great deal of writing but is less easy to do at A level, although they should understand that if they are writing more than drawing or painting, they are probably doing too much. Written notes, annotations and evaluations are all that is needed. They should compare artworks by selecting aspects that are similar or different; they can extract and reproduce particularly interesting qualities or add annotations, helping examiners to understand their visual explorations.

Encourage students to consider what makes particular works

of art interesting to them: are they interested in the concept, lighting, scale, texture, contrast or the use of material, for example? They should make notes on their likes or dislikes about the work; how, when and where it was made; the materials used; whether it was made during a particularly significant time and why it was made. If students are reluctant to write a lot, it is up to them to make sure that moderators can see what they are thinking and how they are analyzing the work of others through visual means.

There is no way around the fact that all students will have to work diligently and for long hours for both GCSE and A level, but every bit of this time could be used in gaining vital marks towards their exam if you have helped them follow a well structured and coherent path that fully addresses all four assessment objectives. Help them look into the relationship between process and product so they will be able to show their understanding in words or artwork. Remind them that every-thing they do – in and outside of lessons – will count towards their exam. For all students, even though sketchbooks are intended to open up their ideas, with the restrictions of the assessment objectives and the need to achieve high grades there is a danger of becoming too prescriptive and not encouraging creativity or imaginative skills. So although you should en-courage your students to plan their journals, they should also take risks and experiment. If anyone appears despondent or de-motivated, put the journals aside and give them big sheets of paper and sticks of charcoal taped to the ends of paintbrushes. Tell them to loosen up and enjoy being creative.

◆ Girls and boys

Be aware that in general girls tend to be better at working in sketchbooks and journals, while boys need to be coaxed to produce the same kind of work that will gain them the required marks. Because of this, if you teach many boys, work to their strengths. While girls are often at ease writing and analyzing, exploring ideas and investigating materials, boys are not always comfortable working in this way. This is why you should encourage all your students to be as bold as they please, perhaps making 3D work, then photographing or sketching and annotating it for their journals. Or suggest that they turn their sketchbooks into the most creative and innovative books they have seen – creating such things as pop-ups, lift the flaps or other kinds of paper engineering. The restrictions of work journals are not always conducive to boys' inspiration, so try to break free from any limitations and allow boys to work 'outside the book'! Keep them looking at a wide variety of images and objects; keep showing them new techniques and innovative ways of working; and constantly encourage them to create new surfaces and explore new concepts, using unusual or unexpected materials.

Effective use of sketchbooks

Students should keep their sketchbooks as free as possible. Although you should keep students informed about the assessment criteria, tell them that it is more important that they enjoy using their journals and fill them with material that stimulates and inspires them. You can always go over the book at a later date, advising them what they should add and where to reach the required criteria. The main thing is to awaken their creativity and allow them to experiment with ideas, materials and methods. Here are some reminders about using sketchbooks or work journals successfully:

- Sketchbooks are visual diaries or journals; as such, they should store personal responses, including thoughts, ideas and experiences – whatever provokes a student's interest visually or emotionally.
- Sketchbooks should be personal and unique; a collection of knowledge, insights, inspirations and artistic skill that no one else has.
- Sketchbooks should be near at all times, so ideas can be jotted down, skills can be tried out and drawings completed whenever the situation allows.
- They should demonstrate the student's investigating and making skills, building confidence as students handle, experiment with and control a variety of media.
- They should demonstrate the student's critical and analytical skills as they enquire into their own work and that of other artists and designers. In this development, students should also learn to evaluate their responses and understand what to leave out as much as what to include.
- Students should explore a variety of ideas. This could include visual notes with brief written comments, evaluations of others' work, sketches, detailed drawings and paintings, work from direct observation and from secondary sources.

- A bit like a scrapbook, sketchbooks can also include evidence collected from around them, such as photographs, objects that catch their eye and other imagery.
- Students should be inventive and experimental with media in their sketchbooks, trying out things they might not have used before.
- Students should develop and extend their art vocabulary in their sketchbooks, using key terms and phrases wherever possible.
- As students work through their sketchbooks, they should gain an understanding of what interests them, self-awareness and self-motivation.
- Sketchbooks should be used as part of the creative process, a journey of exploration; to stimulate and enliven pupils' imaginations and artistic abilities.
- Sketchbooks should show the development of documentation skills, in collecting and recording information.
- Sketchbooks can be constructed by students or bought from a shop or the art department.
- Sketchbooks should show evidence of risk taking and innovation.
- Although sketchbooks do not have to be neat or 'perfect', they do need to be legible and interesting to look at.

Tell students that they need to show progression in their work journals; that each page should carry on from the last but they are also allowed to take wrong turnings, or what the exam boards often call 'imaginative leaps.' Make sure they understand that this simply shows how deeply they have thought about the problem and how much they have explored and experimented. To this end, they should explore ideas with sketches, colour samples, photos, short notes, examples of other artists or designers' work and anything else they can add that shows they are really getting under the surface of an idea or problem. They should be particularly aware that everything in their journal should be original. Even if they copy someone else's work, they should explain what they have learned from it and how they are going to develop their own original work from someone else's ideas or techniques. They should be encouraged to make the pages of their sketchbooks interesting and appealing.

A certain amount of notes should be included on most pages – these can vary hugely. Students should be encouraged to describe their thought processes by writing down their ideas as they work. They should fill their sketchbooks with observational studies from primary sources, use a variety of materials, add photographs and other evidence and, wherever possible, compare and contrast their own studies and ideas with the work of others.

'Sustained investigations' is another phrase often used by the exam boards. It means that students should continue to explore ideas and not 'hop' from one idea and theme to another. In depth and prolonged studies are to be encouraged.

◆ Exam board requirements

Exam boards in the UK make it a mandatory requirement that students keep a work journal. This is to comply with established good practice and to ensure continuity and progression. Work journals are described as a combination of sketchbook and time based record. They should not merely be seen as a sketchbook. The form of the work journal will reflect each student's approach, but in particular the contents must provide evidence of the student's ability to focus on the assessment objectives. Exam boards insist that the journal must contain evidence of students' development of ideas, including reference to the work of others, showing understanding of meanings, contexts and the ability to make skilled judgements, using appropriate images and vocabulary. The work journal is a vital tool in supporting, stimulating and exploring visual ideas. Its use encourages creative thinking and can improve students' general learning skills.

◆ Useful tips for developing students' sketchbooks

From GCSE onwards, if the words sketchbook or work journal do not inspire, try calling them research journals. Sometimes this simple adjustment to the name gives the students the impetus to try several different methods of collecting and analyzing data as well as approaches to interpretation. Remind students that they must show that they have looked at original art in galleries and museums, developed ideas, experimented and made links between their own art and the work of other artists. Here are some further suggestions:

- Prohibit erasers – development should be shown and leaving mistakes is part of this, especially if students explain where they think they have gone wrong.
- Sketchbooks should collect and incorporate a varied range of relevant images and objects, such as tickets, postcards and cuttings.
- Suggest students consider all their senses when recording ideas and impressions, not just sight.

- Encourage the use of viewfinders when looking at other artwork and images.
- If students become 'stuck', tell them to explore textures, materials, colours and so on, rather than worry about the problem. They can return to the problem later.
- Annotation should simply be written notes, clarifying what the student is thinking. Explain that it's their dialogue with moderators, and as such should say what they would say if they could speak to the moderators.
- Above all, emphasize their need to draw from direct observation of primary sources.
- Make clear that annotations should also help them to think constructively.
- Recommend that pages are varied. For instance, some pages should contain detailed drawings or paintings, some should include facts and observations about other artists' work, some should contain small sketches and written notes, some should display collected items and others should feature experiments with materials.
- Things they could consider: mood or atmosphere; composition, perspective and viewpoints; use of materials and techniques; similarities and differences; colour, texture or pattern; abstraction or expression; storytelling.

◆ *Sketchbook assessment*

With reference to assessment for learning, which was discussed in more detail in Chapter 2, sketchbooks are extremely helpful. They are ideal opportunities for you to gain insights into your students' developing skills and how broadly and critically they are thinking. As a result, you may be able to make suggestions for areas of further exploration, which will in turn help them to progress. Marking of sketchbooks should include straightforward suggestions or comments indicating where improvements could be made. Beyond KS3, it's a good idea to write on Post-It notes, rather than writing on the actual pages. Keep an eye on the books as students work and collect them in regularly. Give brief comments on relevant pages and summarize progress at the end. Also speak to pupils about their work to make sure that they know what to aim for and how to modify their work.

Motivating and inspiring, developing creativity and imagination

8

"Attitude is the mind's paintbrush; it can colour any situation," Unknown.

Most art teachers are also art practitioners, so probably more than any other subject they have the opportunity to share their knowledge, skills and passion for their subject. By sharing your own insights, benefits of practical experience and enthusiasm, you will automatically stimulate the majority of your students and enhance their thinking, even beyond the art rooms. Pupils respond to enthusiasm and dedication, a positive attitude and obvious commitment to a subject. If you show your love for the subject, it will occur to most students that it is worth taking seriously. So your attitude alone will help to inspire and motivate – but there are other ways to help students develop their creativity and confidence. Eight characteristics have been identified as major contributors to student motivation in general:

- teacher's enthusiasm
- relevance of the material
- organization of their lessons
- appropriate difficulty level of the material
- active involvement of students
- variety
- rapport between teacher and students
- use of appropriate, concrete and understandable examples.

All eight factors should be the essentials of most art lessons!

Classroom management

Before you can motivate a class you need to have everyone paying attention, so disruptive or reluctant learners need to be dealt with from the start. Methods of discipline and controlling a class are personal and need to be tried and tested. The best approach is to deal with the miscreants swiftly and while everyone else is getting on with a set activity. It is not a good idea to stop the progress of the majority in order to lecture the minority as this not only gives bad behaviour more attention than it deserves, but can also create a negative atmosphere in the room. Disruptive behaviour or attention seeking is usually restricted to a minority, so develop the withering look and speak to them directly and quietly. It can be daunting to face disruptive students, especially in the first months and years of your teaching – refer to school and department sanctions and develop your own strategies for dealing with difficult situations. Similarly, do not keep reminding whole classes of the need to achieve high exam grades or some of your students are likely to become anxious and will not perform well.

Getting lessons underway in a quick and focused manner in order to establish the momentum of the lesson is an essential part of classroom management. Give clear instructions so students are sure of what is expected of them. Guidelines on how each task is to be performed must be specific and well understood. Always make it clear to students what they should be doing, how they should progress through a task or when they should change an activity and how long it should take. Insist on silence when you are explaining anything and make sure that everyone knows what they are doing and what is expected of them before you move on to the next phase of each lesson. Unless everyone is clear about the work, objectives, safety precautions and practical techniques required, they cannot be fully motivated. Consequently, although you need to establish pace, do not move too fast at the expense of understanding. If everyone understands each task and what is expected of them, they will have a platform from which they can develop and gain confidence.

Be clear about your rules within the class and carry out your usual methods for keeping everyone concentrating throughout each lesson but always make sure that the focus of your lesson is art, not discipline. As long as you keep control, maintain consistent expectations and keep encouraging creativity, you will be giving your pupils the best basis for developing their self-belief and uncovering their own resourcefulness.

◆ *Keeping students interested*

As well as your expectations, in order to motivate your pupils, individuals must have expectations of their own. From their first art lessons with you, students need to develop their own aims and intentions. Some do this without conscious effort. They are naturally motivated, curious, interested and willing to learn. Others are less motivated, but can be inspired to work, perhaps to avoid punishment, achieve a high mark or to impress their peers. Some of the most difficult to motivate are those students who worry about what others think of them and try to show that they don't care or wish to show off. The challenge here is to interest them and take their minds off their own preoccupations.

Whether to give or withhold attention is a balancing act that you will have to determine as you get to know individuals. Pupils who are inherently self-motivated help to stimulate others in the class, so it pays to encourage them. In turn, they will consciously or unconsciously encourage others. Often motivation and determination occurs when a project has gone particularly well, which is why it pays to vary materials and activities – to give everyone a chance to do well. The method used to encourage creativity should be used where appropriate. Other than that, if you find students are losing interest or concentration, try breaking up your lesson into several short activities. Giving them a short time span to do something often motivates individuals.

Give students plenty of resources, encouragement, suggestions and guidance. Don't let them plump for the first idea they have. After this, stand back and let them think and work independently. Most learners will start to come up with ideas once they have accepted any restrictions or boundaries and have been given the appropriate tools and materials. Don't forget that students learn in different ways (see Chapter 2), so try to always include a range of different activities to keep them engaged. Having said that, do not beat yourself up because you are not managing to teach all your pupils in their preferred learning styles during each lesson. This would be not only impossible, but unrealistic; if each pupil was taught only in one way individuals would not be able to build up a full range of learning skills. No one has just one learning style and no teacher could manage to meet the specific needs of every child in each class during each lesson. You simply need to use a bit of common sense and intuition. Situations change from class to class and from week to week. Use your awareness of the differences between pupils' learning preferences to help sustain their motivation but realize that there will be times when you might simply need to give them extra support and encouragement.

Some students simply need a bit more reassurance in order to be motivated. Their reasons are many and need not be considered here. An A4 sheet that is useful in helping them to understand whether or not they really need help or can manage by themselves is available to download online. Once they realize that they can get on, many students gain new confidence and so become more motivated.

◆ Resources

The more resources you can surround pupils with, the better for their creative development and learning. By providing them with a varied a range of images, books, artefacts and objects, you will extend their experiences and give them a broader base from which to work. The more they have around them from which to see and learn; the greater their understanding of art and the opportunities they will develop to express themselves. Whether the things they see are objects they are familiar with, a single fact they were not aware of or something they have never looked at before, all will enhance and open up new pathways, fresh attitudes and approaches that might not have previously been considered. Just looking at an object in a new way or noticing a texture in a painting can suggest new ways of thinking, because making connections with ideas, images and information helps to unleash creativity. As you vary your activities, so you should include a variety of learning resources. This is where can never have too much knowledge! Suggesting artists, artefacts or designers can lead your students on to new and unexpected solutions.

◆ Approaches

In the world of work, increasingly (and disappointingly) there seems to be a culture of blame. Aim to avoid this attitude from entering your art room. Give regular, positive and useful feedback that helps pupils believe that they can do well. Research has shown that a teacher's expectations can have a powerful effect on a student's performance. So keep your expectations high but realistic and expect your students to be motivated, hardworking and interested. Expect results that are attainable with effort, but not so difficult that students will give up. Failure to attain unrealistic goals is disappointing and frustrating.

Be adaptable. For instance, if a student wants to make a large Modroc figure, but time and ability preclude this, suggest he or she makes a body part or a relief instead. Give praise wherever possible or offer constructive criticism. Explain where adjustments and improvements can be made and help students evaluate their progress by encouraging them to critique their own work, analyze their strengths and work on their weaknesses. Allowing students to improve their work independently and then give it to you for reassessment is another way you can raise their hopes and confidence. Reassure them that they can think for themselves and achieve success through their own merits, not always from you telling them what to do. All pupils should believe that they can succeed through their own efforts, so when they apply themselves always try to praise their achievements to add to their incentive.

Positive feedback is a great catalyst for inspiration and further motivation. Refer back to strategies for developing thinking skills and when you ask questions give them time to come up with suggestions and answers and don't always tell them how to improve something – let them think around a problem. Try to keep all projects open enough so that students can explore and interpret them from a personal viewpoint and can attain good marks for different levels of achievement. Try to stand back once practical tasks are underway and let your students work more independently. With each class or group, during every lesson, create a positive and open atmosphere and try to make sure that all pupils feel valued in the art rooms. They should know that the art rooms are where they can explore ideas and try out all sorts of materials and notions without being ridiculed. Here are some suggestions to encourage self-motivation:

- Explore and experiment with ideas, materials, tools and techniques. Don't dismiss any ideas or suggestions until you have considered them carefully.
- Take risks with ideas and the use of materials. Learn from your own mistakes.
- Learn as much as you can about different materials, techniques and processes and try out as many as you can.

- Investigate a variety of images and artefacts and use them in unexpected ways or to help to instigate new ideas.
- Study how other artists, craftspeople and designers have worked.
- Develop your skills and fresh ideas by working from firsthand observation and other sources.
- Draw to show that you have looked and understood, and to communicate your own feelings, experiences and ideas.
- Explore and develop ideas using sketchbooks as often as you can.
- Research and investigate to find out as much as you can about concepts surrounding any topic you are working on.

◆ *Communication*

Effective learning in the classroom frequently depends on the teacher's ability to communicate and maintain students' interest. A good communicator will engage pupils in the subject matter; convey a perception of its usefulness; stimulate the desire to do well and boost self-confidence. This is not a straightforward task! Everyone is motivated by different values, needs and desires, so you need to communicate on different levels. Some students are motivated intrinsically – wanting to do well from an inner compunction – while others are motivated extrinsically – through outside factors, such as wanting to avoid confrontation or to gain the approval of others.

Good communication begins with thorough preparation. A well-organized teacher can keep the pace of each lesson going while imparting a great deal of information. Communicating your own enthusiasm is crucial. Students react to who teachers are, what they do and how enthusiastic they are about their subject. Your enthusiasm comes from your own confidence, enjoyment of the subject and pleasure in imparting your knowledge and passion. Develop the ability to ask key questions and stimulate open-ended answers. Maintain sensitivity to students' backgrounds or cultural differences and make sure that you communicate clearly to everyone.

Genuine interest in your students helps here, so try to engage with them on a personal level (to a certain extent) and consider how students will perceive your words. Pay attention to their faces as you speak and check that everyone is listening and understanding. Once you have found out what students' strengths and interests are, try to relate projects to their interests and experiences. Ideas for projects that might be relevant to them could be using the local environment, an event in the news, pop culture, technology or music, for instance. If you can understand their perceptions and viewpoints, you will be halfway to enhancing their interest and motivation in your subject. Fortunately with art, the opportunities to use relevant topics are always there and are often particularly pertinent.

Once you have interacted and established a dialogue with each class or group and with individuals, your next task is to make your students active participants in their own learning. Tell students that they can all succeed and do well in art lessons. For similar reasons, avoid public criticism of anyone's performance in order to keep them enthusiastic and positive about their work. Part of great communication is listening, so always listen to your students and pay attention to their needs, where possible, even when they are not speaking. You can usually see by their work if they are struggling or losing interest, so be ready to offer suggestions or resources that could open up new ideas and inspiration.

◆ Keep them busy

By thinking, making, writing, designing, creating and solving problems, students' natural curiosity becomes awakened. Keep asking questions without giving solutions; offering students opportunities to think for themselves. Introduce class or group discussions and try to encourage interest and participation, even with the quiet ones. Where possible, allow students significant input into their choices of objectives and activities. Students are more motivated if they have some say in what the task is, how it is to be carried out and presented. The more controlling you are, the less motivated learners will be. By feeling that they have some ownership of decisions and activities in their art lessons, they will be more motivated to succeed and show you that they were right. Giving your students autonomy can be as simple as letting them choose what size paper they use or whether or not to work in groups, choosing a partner or selecting their own still life objects from a shelf, or it can be more complex, such as setting their own time limits for a project or grading their own work. When students feel they have power over their work, their efforts and motivation increase.

Students perform best when the level of difficulty is slightly above their current ability level. If the task is too easy, it will promote boredom and may communicate a message of low expectations or they will think that you believe they are not capable of better work. On the other hand, a task that is too difficult may be seen as unattainable, could create anxiety and they might even give up working. One way of determining what is too easy or difficult is to gradually raise the difficulty level of each task as students learn and master activities each week.

◆ *Freedom to develop*

For many years across all subjects, competitiveness in class was encouraged as teachers believed that this spurred learners on. While this can add incentive, intense competition creates anxiety and where possible you should try to reduce students' tendencies to compare themselves to one another. Rather than enhance the experience, this often interferes with learning. In art lessons, where work in progress is evident to all, a certain amount of comparison and so competition cannot be avoided but try to keep it to a minimum. Praise different qualities in all students' work where possible. Frequently remind your pupils that there is no right or wrong way of working and although you have expectations and they have set objectives, there are still many different ways they can achieve this without copying or worrying about others' progress. With this in mind, also avoid any public criticism of students' performance. Help your classes to develop the understanding that mistakes are acceptable and something to learn from; that all artists made or make mistakes and are not ashamed of them. Although you might show exemplar work, again it is essential that this does not make anyone in the class feel inadequate. Try to show work where less able students have made a good effort or tried out something innovative as well as work by students with the greatest aptitude.

Positive feedback wherever and whenever you see effort will build students' self-confidence and so their competence. Recognize sincere efforts even if the end result is not perfect. If a student's performance is weak, tell her or him how to improve. Working through problems, students will experience a sense of achievement and confidence that will increase their willingness to learn. While maintaining your authority, create an art room where students feel they belong and can be themselves. People have a fundamental need to feel connected or related to other people. Students who feel they 'belong' have a higher degree of intrinsic motivation and academic confidence. Art teachers who encourage student participation, who are warm, open, helpful and organized tend to have the most motivated and determined

An extreme close-up dramatizes the T Rex. Subjects that students have chosen for themselves produce the best results. Loreto College, St Alban's, Hertfordshire

students. Supportive teachers who listen, encourage, respond to student questions and show empathy for students tend to achieve the best grades. Here are some strategies that successful art teachers recommend:

- provide students with time to reflect, to mind map and ask questions
- when they are engaged in a practical activity, allow students to talk
- encourage students to eliminate preconceived ideas and to consider problems from unusual angles

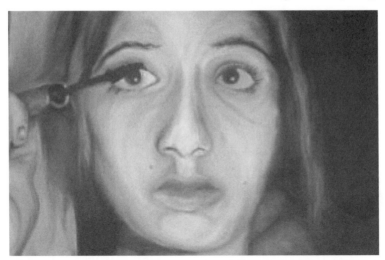

Once students know that they can explore themes that interest them, it is easier to encourage them to try bold and unusual pathways. Year 11 students, Westcliff High School for Girls, Westcliff-on-Sea, Essex

- remind students not to accept the first idea they think of, but always to explore other options as well
- offer encouragement to boost or sustain pupils' engagement
- never criticize their questions, but always respond to them positively
- communicate with students showing that you acknowledge their perspectives
- mutual respect should be one of the art room rules
- allow students the opportunity to feel in control of their learning
- reassure students as they take risks!

◆ *Identify, gather and present*

Visual problem solving and creativity are some of our basic needs and engage people on many different levels. So from the start, many of your lessons will motivate and inspire many students just by being art lessons. As they strive to find answers, pupils develop skills and competences, which in turn help to build confidence and overcome self-consciousness. Art teachers therefore have opportunities to design projects that will motivate pupils to attain new levels of understanding, increase their imaginings and their willingness to take risks. The process of developing this attitude and approach must begin with you showing them how to respond to different creative problems, how to identify solutions and how to develop particular skills.

Although you might show them how to do it, you should also stand back and allow them to do things independently once you have equipped them with the knowledge and understanding. Remain open to any possibilities where you can foster progress and so enhance their abilities to think critically and creatively and to develop their imaginations. Always provide your students with a good grounding from which to explore a visual concept, help them link information, skills and ideas, then give them the freedom and independence to take these further individually. The success and enjoyment students experience in art lessons will remain with many throughout their lives. Millions take up art in later life. This usually stems from humans' inherent desire to be creative. With those desires occurring naturally, it is up to art teachers to cultivate and nurture them from early on.

Teaching and learning 9

Most countries have programmes of study recommended by their respective governments. These are devised to help all teachers focus on a set of shared purposes, values and aims. Some countries' programmes of study are more specific than others. In Britain, for instance, the National Curriculum (which differs slightly in England and Wales) aims focus on the qualities and skills learners need to succeed in school and beyond, across every subject. In England, aims (officially known as attainment targets) in art and design at Key Stage (KS) 3 are:

– investigating and making
– knowledge and understanding.

In Wales, the attainment targets are:

– understanding
– making
– investigating.

The Scottish 5–14 National Guidelines are also similar, with attainment targets as follows:

– using materials, techniques, skills and media: investigating visually and recording
– expressing feelings, ideas, thoughts and solutions: creating and designing
– evaluating and appreciating: observing, reflecting, describing and responding.

These attainment targets should serve as a structure for your lesson plans and you should refer to them as you assess students' progress and achievement. As already discussed, learning objectives must always be met through the lesson activities. By focusing on the learning process rather than the outcome, pupils will be able to justify why they are being asked to do certain things, so it is useful to familiarize them with your own National Curriculum or Guidelines.

Independent learning

It is important to be aware of the differences between independent learning and students working by themselves but not actually learning much, so always consider how they will learn develop through this learning. Lessons with lots of pace and small chunks of different activities are occasionally beneficial, especially if students' attention span is short. Too many of these lessons, however, tend to make students rely on teachers giving them direction and telling them what to do. While you may spend many lessons doing just this, in the majority of your lessons (usually in the middle of a unit of work) you should step back and allow students time to develop thinking skills and methods of self-sufficient working and creative problem solving. As a new art teacher, you might feel that stepping back and allowing your pupils to make their own mistakes means you are somehow not doing your job properly, but in the long run, by planning carefully and giving everyone the tools they need to develop inquiring minds and the determination to succeed, you are doing exactly what you are being paid for! Here are some suggestions to help:

- remind pupils that although you are showing them what to do, they must take responsibility for their actions and develop in their own ways
- if necessary, change seating arrangements to ensure that everyone gets an equal opportunity to work well
- always consider individuals' specific religious or cultural beliefs when planning lessons that encourage the representation of ideas or experiences
- provide clear and unambiguous feedback to pupils to aid further learning
- build on pupils' knowledge, experiences, interests and strengths to improve areas of weakness and give them a chance to progress
- set objectives that are attainable and yet challenging to help pupils develop their self-confidence.

A great deal of independent learning comes from students' natural or intrinsic aptitudes:

- creativity and imagination
- self-expression and perception
- spatial awareness

  – visual aptitude (perception of colour, tone, composition, size, etc.)
  – physical acuity (drawing, hand–eye coordination, etc.).

As you can see, intrinsic aptitudes are inbuilt in individuals, while extrinsic aptitudes need to be learned. These can include:

  – developing powers of description and analysis
  – increasing inter-cultural awareness (icons, practices, symbols)
  – planning and executing art projects
  – developing and supporting arguments and viewpoints
  – collaborative peer working, self-directed learning

◆ *Personal challenges*

The focus of all your lessons should be on the learning taking place and how students are learning, rather than how you are teaching. In order to encourage learning to take place, lessons need to have scope for interesting outcomes. To do this from Year 7 onwards you need to introduce skills, materials and techniques. In this way, you will be giving your classes the tools to develop and strengthen these skills over the next few years.

Enable students to develop by giving them small tasks that mirror some of the work they would do if they took art at GCSE or A level. This could include analyzing an artist's work and responding to this in a personal way. They could learn how visual and spatial qualities can be organized and combined for different purposes by drawing figures in a landscape using one point perspective. Or they could examine Constructivist or Futurist sculpture, for instance, and produce a sculptural work based on similar proportions. Or they could select and manipulate images on computers, modifying a self-portrait, experimenting with stippling, pixilation, softening edges, water-colour effect or high contrast and so on.

To attract and hold pupils' attention, projects should be sufficiently open for them to be able to draw on personal experiences, but not so personal that there is little scope for diversity. Activities should challenge and encourage them to meet the curriculum requirements and explore several ways of working, for example collaborating as a group or working individually. For instance, you might introduce them to the work of the French Impressionists as an opening or introductory project at the beginning of Year 8 (see lesson plan online).

◆ *Developing practical and technical skills*

You need to provide a range of materials and demonstrate various skills, techniques and methods of working in order to encourage students to try different ways of working. Once they are confident with certain techniques and materials, they will be more inclined to take creative risks. In addition, students should be shown different ways to enquire and investigate, such as researching in books, libraries, on the internet, in galleries and museums, and contacting and interviewing artists and designers. From early on, they should be introduced to the idea of considering the work of other artists.

As far as possible, try to keep a positive atmosphere in your lessons. Be open to requests if they are likely to lead on to fresh outcomes. Try to not always be in too much of a rush! If someone wants to learn a new technique and you haven't time in the lesson, find time during a lunch break or after school. A bit of time spent showing students certain skills and techniques is rarely wasted. Always encourage everyone to contribute to discussion and questions. Pepper your enquiries with some easy questions and some more demanding ones. Where possible, pose open, challenging questions that require students to consider, analyze and assess information rather than simply remember it. Make sure that you and the rest of the class value everyone's contributions when questions are asked and discussions are underway. Try different approaches to suit different learning styles and set work that builds on your pupils' own interests and cultural experiences. Monitor the pace of work so that everyone has a chance to learn effectively – some will always be slower than others or inclined to speed through tasks.

Remain flexible about pupils' needs. There are often vast differences between classes, even in the same year groups, and between individual's learning styles within those classes. Make sure that pupils are given the chance and encouragement to demonstrate their competence through various lesson styles and activities. As has been mentioned, you can use the programmes of study on the QCA website (http://curriculum.qca.org.uk/) as they have been written so schools can interpret them in ways that are most beneficial to their particular sets of learners. As long as the concepts in the programmes of study are addressed, the ways in which schools interpret and deliver them can be determined at their discretion; the QCA schemes of work are merely guidance resources. From KS4 and beyond, learning should be based on the relevant GCSE or A level. All accredited qualifications are listed on the National Database of Qualifications (NDAQ), which displays information about each of these qualifications, including the awarding body. The database is available here: http://www.accreditedqualifications.org.uk/index.aspx.

Raising attainment

The point of the National Curriculum is to raise achievement in all subjects and to ensure that all schools offer breadth of study. At KS3, it may be difficult to use a broad range of media or methods with large classes and one short lesson each week. It has, however, been seen that some of the most ambitious art departments at KS3 frequently achieve the highest results at GCSE and A level. It seems to follow, therefore, that offering students more challenging demands at KS3 opens up their understanding, aspirations and confidence.

Brushing up on your knowledge and collecting an extensive range of resources also encourages pupils to develop a good understanding of a wide range of art, giving them more opportunities to develop their own learning. Similarly, artists in residence, study trips and visits to galleries and other places of relevant interest will help to open students' eyes to a greater range of ideas and opportunities.

◆ Disparity in learning

Within every class there will be those who do not want to learn. The experience of learning will always be different for everyone, but some are determined to avoid making an effort. While this happens among both boys and girls, the issue of boys' lack of engagement is often a challenge for art teachers, especially when a certain percentage opt for GCSE art in Year 10 because they believe it will be less demanding than other subjects. Strategies for dealing with this include:

- Recognizing whether you have any disparities in your classes and, if so, what they are.
- Writing down the 'problem' pupils and what you think their issues might be (but be prepared to be proved wrong if necessary).
- Providing greater opportunities for spontaneous, direct

engagement with materials, especially in 3D as many 'difficult' pupils respond well to this.
- Identifying subject matter that is particularly relevant to individuals in the class.
- Emphasizing content over presentation when assessing sketchbooks – boys in general are often discouraged by having to keep these neat and tidy.
- Providing both pupils and parents with accurate up to date information on career opportunities in art and design.
- Considering your class seating arrangements to minimize disruptions. In mixed classes, the boy-girl seating arrangement is usually helpful.
- If disruptive behaviour is a problem, try to have a 'proper' conversation with the individuals concerned and find out if you can what the problem is. Point out the effect their behaviour is having on others and try to work out a strategy or targets.
- If one of the problems is a failure to hand in home or coursework, don't fall into the trap of being lenient. Homework is important and coursework even more so. If you let this slide, students will begin to see you as a 'soft touch' and will avoid doing your work regularly. Address the issue swiftly and firmly. If it continues, tell the parents.

◆ Teach drawing

It may sound obvious, but because of the multitude of requirements of the National Curriculum, many art teachers have reduced the amount of drawing they actually teach. This is a mistake, as there are clear indications that inadequacies in basic drawing skills are a significant factor in underachievement at KS4 and 5. There are many reasons why drawing should be taught thoroughly, so try to find time for this in your lessons and in homework activities. First of all, show pupils that drawing skills can be taught and that these skills need to be practised. Ideas include getting:

- Year 7 students to draw from direct observation, while holding a pencil in different ways and learning about control and effects
- Year 12s drawing life-sized figures using charcoal taped to the end of long brushes
- Year 11 to create still life deconstructions of individuals' personal possessions or sequences of movement
- Year 8 to produce tonal drawings of landscapes in charcoal.

Explain to students that drawing can serve many different

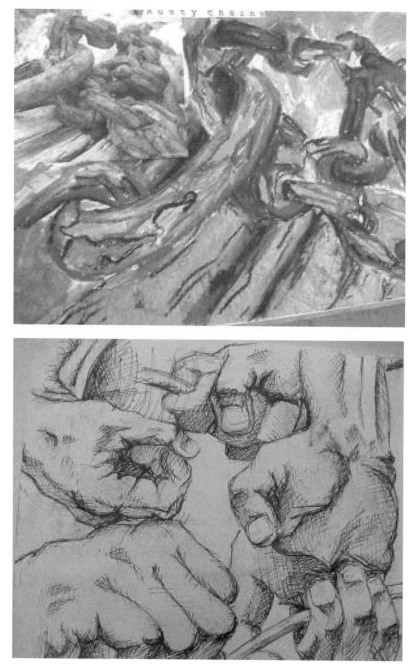

Pencil drawing from direct observation – to be explored further in different materials and scales. Westcliff High School for Girls, Westcliff-on-Sea, Essex

purposes and encourage them to explore drawing in different scales, using a range of media on different surfaces. Show and discuss drawings by other artists. Examples of artists whose drawings often inspire a large leap of learning include: van Gogh, Michelangelo, Escher, Seurat, Bonnard, Matisse, Giacometti, Gruau, Picasso and Leighton.

Aiming high

Research has shown that the most successful art teachers:

- have sound knowledge and understanding of the practice and theory of art
- are aware of pupils' stage of development and plan activities to challenge them
- create a visually exciting environment that feeds pupils' curiosity
- use art room displays as a teaching tool, referring to works on display and showing work that gives pupils the opportunity to observe, contemplate and reflect
- motivate and instil confidence in pupils – let them know that it is safe to contribute and experiment
- plan lessons well, taking account of long-term aims and ensuring their management of pupils, resources and accommodation is proficient
- demonstrate the techniques they expect pupils to use and check through skilled questioning whether they understand;
- teach their lessons briskly, taking a rigorous, but not rigid, approach to standards
- introduce artists and designers as a natural part of the lesson, with emphasis on key terms and vocabulary
- show Year 12 and 13 their high levels of subject knowledge and a prompt grasp of the potential achievement of young people
- if they have experience of art in industry, have an even greater advantage in being able to provide relevant and up to date knowledge and skills;
- have high expectations that accelerate students' progress

◆ *Helping students learn*

You will help your students learn about art by showing them how to explore, analyze, compare, contrast and evaluate their own work and that of other artists, craftspeople and designers from different cultures and periods and then use this knowledge to enrich and inform their work further. The following chart is one way of introducing KS3 pupils to this.

It may not be the easiest thing when you're bombarded with other things to do, but try to be interesting! When you captivate an audience, you help them to focus and concentrate. If you are feeling less than dynamic, make sure that your resources do the motivating for you. As is frequently the case with art teaching,

Thinking and talking about art, craft and design

CONTENT	FORM	PROCESS	MOOD
What is it about? What is its meaning?	How has it been composed, arranged or designed?	How is it made? What is it made of?	How is it affecting me? Why?
Is it based on: • Observation • Memory • Imagination • What makes you think that? • Is it recognizable? • Does it represent something? • Can you tell immediately what it is or do you have to study it closely? • Does it tell a story? • Does it have a use or purpose?	• Is there an overall shape or series of shapes? • Is it a design made of recurring or repeating shapes, lines or forms? • Is there one main texture or a variety of textures, e.g. rough, smooth, thick or thin? • How big is it compared to you?	• What material has it been made from? • Are the materials natural or manmade? • What was the making process? • Can you see signs of how it was made, such as tool marks or brushstrokes? • What kinds of skills would be needed to make it? • Can you tell how old it is? What signs of its age are there? • Do you know what artist, craftsperson or designer make it? Is there a mark or signature?	• How does it make you feel? • Is it surprising or unusual? • Does it remind you of anyone or anything? • Is it something you would like to own? • Is it something you would like to make yourself? • Is it easy to understand or do you need to study it carefully?

this can be completely contradicted by being overly enthusiastic and putting students off! When you are being observed, you will be all-singing, all-dancing, which is right for this type of lesson, but if all your lessons are full of your dynamism (and voice) you will bore your students. Varying activities and pace also includes standing back at times and allowing students to develop their own work at their own pace, with you simply glancing at their progress and occasionally offering a suggestion or word of advice. Another powerful way in which you can interest students and augment their understanding of what artists and designers do is to increase their awareness of career opportunities in the arts. A common mistake of many teachers is to spend a long time explaining the lesson from the front of the room. In order to capture and maintain students' interest, keep your introductions, explanations and instructions brief and concise.

Senior lecturer Leslie Cunliffe, who runs the PGCE art course at the School of Education and Lifelong Learning, University of Exeter, insists that teachers should not merely introduce artists to GCSE or A level students and expect them to assimilate all they should know. He argues that art teachers should always provide students with the ability of 'knowing that' as well as of 'knowing how.' A GCSE candidate, for instance, might show good evidence of knowing how to paint in a style deriving from Matisse's work, using some of his techniques and colours, but might not have interpreted or analyzed the artist's aims or understood the underlying culture that surrounded Matisse in nineteenth century Catholic France. It is up to you to help students understand the whole picture, not just what they see.

◆ *Accelerating learning and pride*

Colour accelerates learning, retention and recall by 80 per cent; improves comprehension by 70 per cent; and increases willingness to read by 80 per cent. Proof enough to display colourful posters, artwork and information around the room or to use colourful images as introductions to each new topic. In the same way, assist learning by celebrating students' artistic achievements in displays of their work. This gives positive feedback to students and staff and encourages further motivation and progress. Already mentioned, displays of students' work within the department and around the school is vital for self-pride, but the recognition of effort and achievement in prize and award giving is also important; whether this is just in school assemblies or in front of parents, governors and other guests at more eminent occasions, such as annual prize giving.

If you can, look out for and enter students' work in local or national competitions, but always clear this with your head of department first. Some heads of department are delighted for staff to take responsibility for such things, while others prefer to keep students' work within the school. Local libraries and councils often run art competitions, so ask around and see what possibilities there are. Even if they don't win anything, just to exhibit alongside other schools can be extremely motivating.

◆ Making sure the right students choose art

Try to make sure that the students who opt for your subject do so for the right reasons. When you tell interested students about GCSE and A level, show them the amount of work they will have to do and explain the various areas of knowledge and understanding they have to cover. If possible, invite a couple of current GCSE students to speak to KS3 pupils and to show them their work. Once you have built up the department's reputation for hard work and solid, thorough output, most students will be aware of the demands on time and intellect necessary in art. There is no point selling art as a fun and enjoyable subject or this is all potential students will understand, and when taking the subject these students will be the ones who do not produce sufficiently in depth or extensive work.

Show folders of GCSE work to Year 9 students and from the start of KS3; make your high expectations apparent to all students. In primary school, art is often the fun and relaxing subject that they do when the academic subjects are finished for the day. Although art is uplifting and enjoyable, you must make it clear to your students that it is considerably more demanding than they might have previously considered. KS3 is the time to lay down foundations for this, developing students' understanding of how to think and work – and how much they need to do. If you can, invite past A level students back with folders of their current work at universities or work that they did during their A level course at school, and ask them to talk to current students or even to run a workshop with them.

◆ Broadening output

From Year 7 onwards, set regular homework to increase the amount of work that students do for you. Make sure that it underpins and advances all they have been learning and mark it regularly. Commonly, departments in which homework plays an important part find that their results are significantly enhanced. Although you should mark work regularly, group marking, where students spread out their homework on a table and discuss it, has benefits. Students are able to evaluate the successful features of their own and others' work and so will be motivated to do their best, knowing their peers will be looking and making comments about their work. At least from KS4 onwards, incorporate gallery visits to broaden students' learning experience. One of the most successful methods in helping students to develop a wider visual awareness is to encourage them to consider content, form, process and mood when looking at any piece of art, whether it is their own or the work of others. Encourage the use of sketchbooks in the gallery and give them instructions such as:

- look all around you and identify aspects of the gallery that inspire you
- consider the title of your theme/topic/unit at all times
- don't waste this opportunity, but make full use of your time
- complete ten pages of your sketchbook
- when you see a work of art that you think may be of value to you, sketch it, annotate it, name the artist, describe what it is made of and so on
- if possible, buy postcards and other visual imagery from the gallery shop to use to bolster your coursework or preparatory studies
- make your sketchbook exciting; later on, add to what you have done in the gallery
- always consider the assessment objectives:

◆ *Art GCSE assessment objectives explained*

AO1: Record observations, experiences and ideas in forms appropriate to intentions

Make notes, mind maps, drawings, colour studies and take photos to record whatever you find, think about, decide upon or look at in relation to the topic. These could be in the form of a work journal, design sheet or storyboard, whatever is appropriate.

AO2: Analyze and evaluate images, objects and artefacts, showing understanding of context

Try to understand meanings, make judgements and comparisons of artworks. Be aware of the time, place and reasons they were made.

AO3: *Develop and explore ideas using media, processes and resources, reviewing, modifying and refining work as it progresses*
Use what is available to help you to explore the topic, e.g. pictures, ideas, information. Develop your ideas, creating and experimenting with different art materials and techniques. Keep considering what you are doing, making alterations and improvements as you go.

AO4: *Present a personal response, realizing intentions and making informed connections with the work of others*
Produce your own, individual work, as you have planned. The ideas and skills gained from looking at the work of others should be used to help your outcome.

◆ *Developing practical, technical and critical skills*

Critical thinking skills can be developed particularly effectively in art lessons. Thinking critically is a natural aspect of creative subjects and, in turn, it expands and increases creative abilities. Help students to form enquiring attitudes by encouraging them to identify creative problems; ask relevant questions; plan and research; anticipate and improve upon ideas. In addition, during art lessons that extend their abilities in collecting, classifying, sorting, comparing, contrasting and analyzing, they will learn how to process information. Constantly introduce key vocabulary and help them to shape their own opinions, judgements and actions and to make decisions from given evidence. In doing this, you are giving them the tools to reason and evaluate. Finally, you will foster their creativity by making them aware of ways they can use their imaginations, generate fresh ideas and apply practical and technical skills they have learned and practised. Help students to consider what they are learning in a broader sense by asking questions. A helpful A4 question sheet is available online that can be downloaded, printed out and handed out before or at the start of the visit.

Throughout each project, remind students of the objectives to keep them focused on the task. By encouraging their development of a variety of practical art skills and different disciplines, somewhere along the way you will interest everyone, even the most reluctant learners. As soon as you see when and where particular students' interests have been engaged, praise their efforts and make a note to try out similar topics, treatments or techniques. Try to foster the understanding that mistakes can be positive as we learn from them, and anything learned can be used to create something better.

AS/A2 assessment objectives – student sheet

This is a checklist to help you make sure that you cover all the assessment objectives for this subject. For each box, be honest with yourself and only tick the boxes if you really mean it. Where you have not ticked any boxes, go back and fill in the gaps in your work.

AO1   *Record observations, experiences, ideas, information and insights in visual and other forms, appropriate to intentions*
Did I:
Produce a range of ideas in my work journal/sketchbook? ☐
Record with sketches and detailed drawings? ☐
Select and organise my work? ☐
Draw from direct observation (primary sources)? ☐
Draw from secondary sources? ☐
Take relevant photos? ☐
Experiment with media? ☐
Produce imaginative responses? ☐

AO2   *Analyse and critically evaluate sources, such as images, objects, artefacts and texts, showing understanding of purposes, meanings and contexts*
Did I:
Visit a gallery or museum? ☐
Interview an artist? ☐
Research in books? ☐
Research on the internet? ☐
Study art and craft at first hand? ☐
Understand other artists' work and show this in writing or artwork? ☐
Use key vocabulary to explain artists' meanings and intentions? ☐

AO3   *Develop ideas through sustained investigations and exploration, selecting and using materials, processes and resources, identifying and interpreting relationships and analyzing methods and outcomes*
Did I:
Persistently work through one or more ideas, experimenting and taking creative risks? ☐
Try out a wide variety of materials and methods? ☐
Examine, choose and use a variety of materials and methods? ☐
Study and explain different, relevant styles and approaches? ☐

AO4   *Present a personal, coherent and informed response, realizing intentions, and articulating and explaining connections with the work of others*
Did I:
Link my work and ideas with the work of others? ☐
Explain, through artwork and/or writing, how I have made links with the work of others and created my final piece? ☐
Produce a logical, thoughtful, personal final piece, linking many of my previous ideas? ☐

Some students will need quite a bit of help to begin with, whether this is at the beginning of Year 7, the beginning of a new project or at the start of GCSE art. Help them decide what and where to research; suggest working methods and help them to choose suitable materials to work with. There will be a time when even the neediest pupils will be able to work independently if you give them a solid grounding and then gradually step away. With your demonstrations, the materials and resources you provide and the encouragement you give them, all students will extend their practical and technical skills. Help them expand their abilities in both traditional and contemporary approaches, encouraging the use of both traditional and new media. When you offer a broad range of materials, there will always be something that suits everyone and encourages participation and endeavour.

It is important that you keep students focused on task and you can only do this by stimulating them with topics and themes that mean something to them. Allowing students to research a topic, produce the work for it and then present their responses to the rest of the class can help them to see their own work from a different perspective and will allow them to develop in new ways. Only do this if you are sure that no one in the class will be intimidated – some pupils will be far too shy to gain any benefit from this approach. Whatever you do, always aim to keep pupils extended and working to the best of their abilities. If you see anyone 'coasting' or losing interest, change their task, teach them a new skill or suggest they try something else and move them in a new creative direction.

◆ Investigating and developing work

Among many other things, students are to be taught to 'develop understanding of the work of artists, craftspeople and designers, applying this to their own work'. This ensures that they become knowledgeable and informed about art and artists, considering others' work in connection with their own. The selection of artists, craftspeople and designers, therefore, should be as broad as possible, including a variety of genres and styles from the past and present and from a variety of cultures. The importance of having a large variety of resources has already been mentioned several times in this book to help students learn about the methods, meanings and approaches of other artists. In turn, they will develop a variety of ways of looking and considering how they work in relation to others. This doesn't usually happen instantly and so should be nurtured in KS3, built into lessons and homework. By the time they reach KS4, you need to push this by giving them plenty of examples of artists, craftspeople and designers to look at from different cultures, backgrounds, eras, purposes and working methods. The trick is to introduce them to good habits early on and to keep reinforcing these. If this aspect is handled well, analytical skills will become integral to their development, along with intuitive skills, as they learn how to portray expression and emotion.

Educational visits

Educational art visits are essential for students' progress and wider understanding. Whether you take a group to a local area for sketching or to a major art gallery, all experiences outside the art rooms are enriching but can be made more so by the way you treat each trip. The habit of looking and seeing critically should start in the classroom and will further students' abilities to interpret and understand, in visual terms, the world around them. Being taken on visits outside the school environment broadens horizons and outlooks.

Difficulties and issues

Due to budget and timetable constraints, bad press, lengthy paperwork and concerns about planning sufficiently for health and safety risks, school visits are not organized as often as they used to be. The NUT website states:

> 'Teachers are now also very conscious of the time-consuming burdens which they must shoulder without the additional burdens of organizing and participating in those school trips which are not obligatory. The voluntary school trip cannot now have priority over these other responsibilities.'

So of course, any educational visit needs to be considered carefully before you plan something. They are hugely rewarding and inspiring for both pupils and teachers, however, and can inspire or rejuvenate even the most jaded attitudes.

Due to the many issues, it is not advisable to undertake visits on your own during your first couple of years of teaching, but organizing one may be a task you are given to be undertaken with an experienced member of staff. Most groups are too large anyway for you to accompany them alone. Individual schools have different procedures for the organization of visits, so make

128

sure you know who is the right person to speak to and whether or not it is your responsibility to book the gallery or museum and write the letter home, or whether this is the job of someone else.

Planning a visit

Plan your visit before you go in as much detail as possible. The DfES recommends you take one adult for every 15–20 pupils in Year 7 onwards on visits to local sites, walks and museum or gallery visits, so ask parents to accompany you if you cannot take a sufficient number of staff. (And try to politely make sure that everyone takes some responsibility – parents are not having a free trip! They should be helping to supervise and organize students.) Visit the site if you can before you go, to see the facilities as well as whether particular works are on display or if they are on loan or have been moved. If you cannot make a prior visit, check out the website, which should have plenty of information. Plan where you will allow pupils to go, as they should not be left unsupervised at any part of the day. Produce a full costing of the transport and entrance fees. (Include a calculation of the minimum amount of 'voluntary contribution' needed to make the visit viable.) Complete a risk assessment and explain this to the designated member of the senior management team.

Make sure that students know what their meal arrangements are going to be in advance and let the school canteen, if you have one, know how many students will be out. Let the person responsible for cover lessons know which teachers will be out on the day and what lessons need to be covered. Make sure that you leave suitable lesson plans and any other instructions in an appropriate place.

Decide what you will be taking your students to see or what they will be concentrating on during the visit and account for the entire time there – even incorporate a timed visit to the gallery or museum shop. On the visit, you will need to take such things as first aid kit, spare sketchbooks, paper, clipboards and pencils. You should remember to take bags for rubbish if you're on a coach or train; a camera; a mobile phone per staff member (with one number left in the school office in case of emergencies) and student evaluation and health forms. Provide group lists to each member of staff accompanying you. Register students frequently, such as: on the coach, off the coach, in the gallery, before leaving and once on the coach again. Be mindful of health and safety requirements during the visit, details of which can be found on the following site: http://www.rospa.com/safetyeducation/schooltrips/part1.htm.

Keep the visit fairly selective, focusing on the topic you are about to cover or are currently working on, or specific areas that are especially relevant to what they are learning in class. Wherever you are going, always introduce some background information beforehand, explaining why you are going there and what you expect them to get out of the visit. Many museums, galleries and other suitable places have educational pages on their websites with useful information, usually with connections to the National Curriculum and often with free resource materials. Many places also have their own risk assessments for school visits, which will ease your workload considerably.

Many schools take art students on extended visits, which include overnight stays abroad. All the above issues need to be considered in these situations, but you need to be even more mindful and vigilant over your organization and student health and safety. Make as many lists as you need and delegate only when you are sure that the other adult will take responsibility for the task and plan thoroughly. The responsibility and preparation will be worth it!

During a visit

A visit is meant to be a treat as well as a rewarding part of the students' education. So consider how you will create a good balance between enjoyment and hard work. Many pupils enjoy visiting museum or gallery shops for instance, so let them know that if they complete seven drawings, say, or three-quarters of the task you have set them, then they will be able to spend 15 minutes in the shop. (For large groups, stagger these visits with a responsible adult or two supervising.)

Your visit might be sketching in a local area or visiting a historical site or area that fits in with a current unit of work, or it might be a gallery or museum visit. The latter are the most popular for art students. It's extremely beneficial for them to see works of art at close hand and not just reproductions. Seeing the scale and textures of works and being able to compare them to other works nearby, as well as understanding them in the context of both the gallery with sympathetic lighting and other works of similar themes or from the same movements, are invaluable. Students should also learn how to behave in such situations and gain pleasure from the experience so they repeat it throughout their lives.

◆ *Forming ideas and opinions*

Everyone's response to a piece of art is different, influenced by personal background, experience and prior knowledge. It is important from the start that you establish that there are hardly any 'wrong' answers when considering art and there is no single way to look at or interpret it. There are some correct facts, but these may not be essential to gaining meanings or insights from the work. We know a lot about art through what the artists themselves have said or written, but much of our views and beliefs stem from the way we see things as individuals. Most artists make observations about their lives and times, but often their work is also about individual viewers' perspectives and how people perceive what they have created. For this reason although you must adhere to the restraints of being in a public place, you should create an environment whereby students feel comfortable in engaging with original art or craft and in voicing their opinions and interpretations, as well as considering others' points of view. Tell them that everybody's considered opinion may be valid.

When at a gallery, museum or other similar venue, before they read a text relating to a work of art, tell pupils to try to gather clues from it, by studying the materials, shapes, arrangement of elements, size and so on. They should work like detectives, trying to find out as much as they can about each work by considering 'clues' such as these. Their responses will provide vital starting points for discussion, which can lead on to making connections between the works they see and their own works back at school. One of the most important components of GCSE and A level is that students should make links between their own art and the work of other artists. So you will need to give them guidelines of what to do when there, how they will work and how much they are expected to produce on the visit and back at school. For Key Stage (KS) 3 pupils, will you give them worksheets or will you set a drawing exercise? Is work to be completed at the site or venue or will you give them more time to work on it before handing it in? Perhaps you are starting an activity in the gallery, location or on supporting topics you have already been working on in class. Whatever use you intend to make of the visit, you will be giving pupils the opportunity to understand and investigate with greater insights than they would have had if they had remained at school.

◆ *Looking at art*

Before they embark on the work you have prepared, try to find out from individuals what they think of a particular artwork. Explain from the start that it is not enough to simply say they like or dislike a work of art. They must give reasons and describe why they feel like that. Try to show them the different methods of looking and considering artworks. These include looking in order to analyze the content, artist's intentions and purposes, and to understand how something was created; then there is looking to assess the qualities of the work that each individual finds interesting or compelling or particularly relevant to their own work. Finally, looking to render it in a drawing or sketch is another way to analyze the work's structure and way that it was made. Explain to pupils that their initial reactions to a work of art will probably be entirely different from their considered opinion once they have looked at it in all these different ways. To assist their observations and understanding, you could give your group sheets with the following prompts that they have to fill in while there:

Visual (*What is your first reaction to the work? What did you notice first?*)

Emotional (*How does it make you feel – for example disturbed, calm, happy or angry?*)

Memory/experience (*Does the work remind you of anything? Does it have any personal connections?*)

Value/appreciation (*Do you like or dislike the work? What reasons do you have for your opinion? Find out more about the work and/or the artist. Do you still feel the same way about it?*)

Or you could give them a checklist of questions, such as the list given online covering subject and meaning, object and form, processes, influences and personal responses.

By encouraging students to engage with works of art from a variety of sources and cultures, you will help them to analyze in greater depth, and so form broader opinions and gain further insights into meanings and methods. This will have a valuable impact upon their own work as they compare the way artists have explored similar themes or used a similar process in an unusual or exciting way. Some further starting points for discussions that can be expanded upon once back in the classroom are given in a table online.

◆ *Activities*

While with your GCSE or A level groups you might simply tell them to explore their personal path with drawings, annotations and other investigations; KS3 pupils will need a firmer structure. Having said that, don't assume that KS4 and 5 students will know what to do. Before the visit, make sure that you have spoken to them all about what they are looking for and what they might get out of the visit. For instance, most will want to draw from works of art, learning from the composition, scale, technique and materials used by making notes about aspects they might not remember once back in class. They should also write how their opinions or attitudes about the work changed once they had started to draw it; how the work relates to other works in the same room; what unexpected colours or materials have been used; can the work be summed up in terms of patterns or shapes? What is the atmosphere or feeling of the work?

Using sketchbooks in galleries provides opportunities to make annotated drawings of artworks. This can help pupils at all secondary levels in their thinking processes beyond the actual gallery visit. By mapping a composition briefly in sketch form and highlighting key features, such as colour, textures, scale and atmosphere, pupils can quickly gather information that they might not otherwise remember.

A five minute introduction to looking at a work of art will act like a warm up exercise and will help students to learn how they observe things. Tell them to look at a work of art for a minute and then spend another minute drawing their initial impression of the work, capturing it in as few lines as possible. A further minute should be spent looking once again at the work and a final two minutes spent embellishing their initial sketch with further ideas, observations and impressions. From this, ask them to reflect on what they considered to be the most significant part of the artwork and to consider why. They should then think about other aspects of the work and how these aspects add to or detract from the entire piece. In this way, you are encouraging pupils to become reflective about their observations and thinking. If looking at 3D work, including sculpture and installations, tell pupils to draw firstly only the shapes around the artwork rather than the art itself and secondly only the artwork. They should then compare their two drawings. For KS3 classes, you could give them a theme, according to your current or future schemes of work and ask pupils to find three works relating to the theme. Each work should take at least a full page of their sketchbooks – they should draw aspects of it and make notes about it, explaining how it relates to the theme.

Another structure could be five minutes orientation; 15 minutes discussing one work of art; 30 minutes activity in small groups; and ten minutes plenary, discussing what they have done.

Here are some further suggestions of gallery or museum activities for KS3 students:

- *Movement* (can be started on the visit): Many artists have looked at the challenge of representing movement or a sequence of actions in a nonmoving work of art. Artists could include: Degas, van Gogh, Muybridge, Delaunay, Bomberg, Turner, Giacometti, Richter or any of the Futurists. Calder and Tinguely, for example, although slightly different as kinetic artists, are also worth looking at. Students are to find two works by artists that show movement. They are to make notes, including the following:
  - artist (name, nationality, dates)
  - title and subject
  - materials used
  - how has the artist shown movement?
  - what colours, shapes, marks or materials particularly convey the sense of movement?
  - make a sketch of the each of the works.
  After the visit, students are to explore movement and how to portray it. Discuss what they saw in the gallery and then they should mind map different sorts of movement (e.g. wind, rain, machines, figures running or dancing, birds flying, animation or computer games) and how they might show this in a static work of art. After trying out six small ideas, they are to create one major artwork, conveying some form of dynamism or activity. Homework activities could include designing packaging for shampoo or trainers that captures the sensation of movement, and designing a flick book showing movement.
- *Renaissance art* (can be a continuation of a unit of work already underway or can be started on the visit): In small groups, give students some time to look at works completed during the

Renaissance period. Each group should compile a list of six words to describe aspects of the art (e.g. precise, religious, linear, figurative, wealthy, important or large). They are to discuss (quietly) what the artworks have in common. Is there a shared style, subject, medium or attitude? Are there stories behind the works? Are there symbols or hidden meanings? Within each group, students are to select three works and make notes about them, answering the above questions and adding some further information, such as: Does the work look precious? Who commissioned it? In what ways is it realistic or not? Does it record how people lived or was it contrived to convey a certain message? Have the images been used to provoke religious belief and knowledge? How has perspective been shown? (Look for linear and aerial perspective.)

Back in class, students are to plan and produce a work of art that will communicate with a future society about them, their class and their community or beliefs. They are to select materials and use techniques that they believe will show this to the best effect. They should also choose some of the techniques they saw in the works in the gallery, such as linear perspective or draped fabric, for instance.

- *Identity* (this could be a continuation of a unit of work already underway or can be started on the visit): This activity works well if you are going to a gallery where figures feature in the works (this could be painting, photography or sculpture). Artists could include: Holbein, van Gogh, Rembrandt, Sherman, Beaton, Cameron, Rodin, Blake, Freud, Modigliani, Velázquez, Warhol, Picasso, Renoir, Gainsborough, van Dyck or any of the German Expressionists. Before the visit, ask pupils to divide a page of their sketchbooks into four. In each quarter page, they should write words to describe how they are seen by:
  - their parents, grandparents or carers
  - their brothers, sisters or cousins
  - their friends
  - their teachers

Discuss the differences that there might be in portraits painted by strangers, by friends or family or themselves (self-portraits). What is our identity? Is it how we perceive ourselves or how others see us? Do we have symbols that identify us – is there something we do (a habit) or carry or wear that symbolizes us? Discuss group (e.g. school logo) and individual symbols (e.g. glasses). If someone was going to portray you in a work of art, what would you prefer, e.g. a video, painting, photo or sculpture? They should look at a selection of portraits and works with people in and decide, in groups, how identity is communicated visually. Armed with ideas, they will be ready to look in the gallery.

Once there, in small groups, students are to find four works that feature people. In their sketchbooks, they should make notes about the work, artist, person portrayed, date, materials and how they think the person felt about his or her representation. Does the date, occupation or gender of the person have any significance? Are there any symbols that add to the information you receive from the work? Would you like to know the person portrayed? Has the artist done a good job, i.e. is the identity 'rounded' or does it seem biased? Explain. Make visual notes and sketches of the four works. Back in class consider what views your artists were showing. How are clothes, body language, composition, style and materials shown and used to create a particular image? Students are to:

- produce four self-portraits showing different aspects of their identities
- sketch two family members or friends relaxing
- take photos of themselves or people they know
- produce an expressive work showing more than just superficial appearance

• *Investigating artists' marks* (this works well as an activity in the gallery and can be extended back at school or kept as a one off): Students are to find a 2D artwork and using pencil, pen or coloured pencils, make visual notes about the marks the artist has used to show differentiation of areas and objects, for instance buildings, sky, leaves, chairs, happiness or anger. They should fill a page with these marks – exaggerating them if necessary – and then find another work by the same or another artist. They should make a copy of the second work, using the expressive marks they have been studying from the first work.

Language for art

A wide range of relevant vocabulary will help students engage with the work. In equipping pupils with the appropriate language to discuss works of art, you will help them to express their thoughts and feelings with greater depth and appreciation. Key vocabulary at the back of their sketchbooks can be added to throughout each year in KS3. You could produce a suitable vocabulary sheet for each year group or you could add a detailed art terms vocabulary to the school intranet. Here are a few words to help students describe what they see on school visits (table also available online):

Composition
Foreground – front
Background – back
Rhythm – flowing
Abstract – non-figurative
Figurative - figures
Stable – static
Dynamic – moving
Juxtaposed – next to each other
Triptych – three in a row
Expressionist – emotional
Iconic – religious/famous
Tranquil – serene/calm

Line
Convoluting – twisting
Converging – coming together
Spiral – twisting
Hatched – short, directional lines
Chevron – 'v' shapes
Crosshatching – criss-crossed
Horizontal – side-to-side
Vertical – straight up
Diagonal – corner-to-corner

Texture
Impasto – thick paint
Abrasive – rough
Sheen – gleam, not shine
Fluid – smooth, moving
Matt – not shiny
Pliable/malleable/yielding – soft and springy
Rigid/durable/inflexible – hard
Jagged/coarse – rough

Tone
Chiaroscuro – contrasting light and dark
Opaque – not see-through
Translucent – semi-see-through
Transparent/lucid – clear
Gradated – gradually lighter or darker
Sculptural – is or looks 3D

Colour
Harmonious – calm
Discordant – clash
Complementary – opposites on the colour wheel
Primary – red, blue and yellow
Secondary – green, violet and orange
Tertiary – mixture of three primaries or one secondary and one primary
Warm – reds and oranges
Cool – blues and greens
Receding – appears to go back
Advancing – appears to come forward

Form
Angular – edgy
Spherical – round
Cuboid – 3D square
Elliptical – oval shaped
Anthropomorphic – resembling humans
Pediment – triangular section of a temple roof
Entablature – part of a building above columns and below roof
Trapezoid – four-sided

Materials
Encaustic – pigment mixed with wax and applied while hot
Mosaic – art made of small pieces of coloured glass or stone
Pastel – coloured chalk
Watercolour – pigment mixed with water to make paint
Ceramic – hard, brittle material made by baking
Glaze – a smooth, glossy surface

Technique
Tone – light and dark in an image to create a sense of depth
Painterly – energetically painted
Aggressive – energetic marks
Stippling – dabs, dots
Wet-on-wet – wet paint over wet to make soft edges
Dry brush – paint with little moisture
Etched – scratched by acid
Pointillist – dots

Homework and worksheets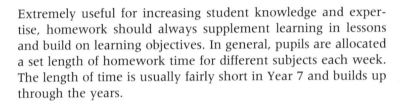

Extremely useful for increasing student knowledge and expertise, homework should always supplement learning in lessons and build on learning objectives. In general, pupils are allocated a set length of homework time for different subjects each week. The length of time is usually fairly short in Year 7 and builds up through the years.

Planning and setting

Commonly, secondary schools set about 20 minutes of art homework per week in Year 7, increasing to about 30 minutes in Year 8 and 40 minutes in Year 9. This rises considerably at GCSE and A level. For practical tasks, ease of marking and handing in during a weekly lesson, many art teachers find it is more practical in Key Stage (KS) 3 to set art homework fortnightly so the working time is doubled up. You set the work in one lesson, collect it in the following week, mark it and then hand it back in the next lesson. Not all schools allow this however, so you need to plan accordingly.

Make sure that when you write schemes of work (SoW), you include details of any homework – when it will be set, what it will entail and how long it will take. Make sure that all homework supports any current project and that tasks are not merely 'tacked on' to a topic, but actually increase relevant knowledge or skills. Homework should extend students' learning and help to fulfill set learning objectives. As such, it should either follow on or prepare students for particular areas of study. For GCSE and A level groups, it is a good idea to have a regular date, say the first Thursday of every month, when they hand in their sketchbooks. They do not have to have completed a task, it just means that you can keep an eye on progress regularly and spot any potential wrong turnings or promising ideas emerging.

◆ *Variety*

Some homework will naturally take longer than others. It is difficult and not always appropriate to set homework of exactly the same time length each time. Activities are different, so the length of time spent on them will frequently differ slightly, although care should be taken to try to keep the timing compliant with allocated homework periods. The time you plan to should fit in with the homework policy of your school, although generally anything less than half an hour will result in fairly superficial work and many students will often take much more time than this, even if you plan for it.

Just as you incorporate variety in your lessons, so you should include a mixture of activities and tasks in the homework you set. Some tasks, for instance might require students to research, some might need them to collect materials and others might ask them to make or produce something. Homework should be challenging and should appeal to different learning styles, but it is less easy to accommodate individuals when they are taking the task away to do without your guidance. Most students will interpret any homework in their own way, which means that some will naturally make more effort and others will try to get away with doing little.

For KS3, practical work can sometimes be produced on separate paper rather than sketchbooks and once completed displayed around the room for a couple of weeks, space permitting. When on show like this, some will be encouraged to try harder! Minimum effort often looks weak or embarrassing. On the other hand, some make good efforts and their work still does not look as impressive as others. Gauge your classes to accommodate this – there is no point in humiliating or upsetting diligent or earnest students. Aim to design individual homework tasks to either contrast with or complement the work that was undertaken during the previous lesson.

From Year 10 onwards, homework is often necessarily quite extensive and can be considerably time consuming. Be aware of how much work you set and try not to overwhelm students or cause anxiety in your efforts to encourage them to attain high grades. Before students opt to take art and design at GCSE or A level, make it clear that there will necessarily be a heavy workload but that no time working in art and design is ever wasted.

◆ *Making homework straightforward*

Homework should be set during a lesson, allowing time for questioning and for notes to be made in planners. It should not be tacked on to a plenary or called out as the class is leaving the room. Try to incorporate a calm few minutes during the lesson to introduce the homework, explaining and demonstrating what is required where necessary, just as you would for the lesson. This might be at the beginning or near the end of the lesson – it usually depends on the topic and tasks. Often a visual example that you or a student have made will help pupils to understand clearly the type of thing you are looking for. You need to explain the task as clearly as possible, so there is no ambiguity or confusion.

Bear in mind that some pupils will not have many materials at home and some will not have access to books or the internet. Make it known that there are options in school if anyone has difficulties in obtaining necessary materials to complete homework. If you have students who do not have access to necessary materials, a good idea is to have a box filled with essentials they can borrow, such as pencils, coloured pencils, pastels, scissors and so on, but for books or a computer, recommend that they use the school or public libraries. For the borrowing of items, include a notebook in the box where each pupil writes his or her name, form and the date on which the item(s) were borrowed.

◆ *Homework structure*

Structure homework so that students have to explore ideas, research, make decisions or create something. Homework is an opportunity for students to work completely independently of you, so make sure that everyone understands what you are asking them to do and then they can take responsibility for the progress and outcome of their own work. The aim is to promote individual approaches and the development of personal ideas and explorations. Be careful not to be too prescriptive or the work could all look the same. Allow a certain amount of choice and diversity so individuals can decide for themselves how to tackle the task. The intention is that they will go beyond what you anticipate, rather than fall short of it. (Make sure you are sensitive here: if a student has taken risks and experimented, but the work has not met his or her intentions, reward the effort nonetheless.)

Although homework should either progress from or prepare for class work, it should also include separate tasks and be seen as an opportunity for students to demonstrate self-directed skills beyond the art room and it should help them to develop further. Homework tasks should be appealing so that students are encouraged to make an effort. Never forget to give them the learning objectives or your assessment criteria, in order to help them make the right sort of effort.

◆ Ideas for homework

Homework should derive from your SoW so will necessarily be constructed to match your programmes of study. There are a number of general suggestions that could be adapted to suit your units of work available online.

◆ Firsthand and secondhand research

In order to help students think around a subject that you might set for homework, they must research. All students need to know the difference between firsthand and secondhand sources.

Clearly, most will not be able to visit art galleries for their homework, but gallery and museum websites are in the main well-designed and provide excellent secondary sources. Similarly, books from the art room and school and local libraries provide invaluable information, as do art magazines and relevant articles in newspapers. Older students should be encouraged to collect anything that they think might be relevant: from newspaper images and articles, to leaflets from art galleries, to photocopies or notes made from books. Arts programmes on television or DVDs are also useful secondhand sources. Remind all students that the internet is a wonderful resource, but should never be relied upon completely – information is not always true and they should never copy directly from it.

For firsthand research, they could take photos, make sketches and annotations. It's a good idea to collect objects for the art department for students to use as primary sources for drawing from direct observation: these can be all sorts of things, from shells, stones and pieces of bark, to bottles, old toys and clothing. It might be that you can work out a system whereby they can borrow some of these things for their homework. Always emphasize the need to work from primary source material and get your students into the habit from Year 7.

Worksheets

Not to be relied upon in 'normal' art lessons, worksheets nonetheless have an important role to play in the art department. If you and colleagues can amass a collection of worksheets and store them, systematically and clearly labelled, you need never be caught out in a tricky situation. Paper-free on the computer is helpful, only printing those you need when you need them, or displaying one on the interactive whiteboard for everyone to read. If a colleague is absent or suddenly called away, if you need cover for your lesson or an extension activity for a speedy or able student, when a class is moved to a room other than an art room – all these reasons and more are when worksheets are invaluable.

Some teachers sneer at them but they can be extremely versatile and useful, provided they are not relied upon too often, nor used as a substitute for imaginative teaching. Worksheets should be written to enhance pupils' experience and to help them to progress in areas that complement the National Curriculum. Ideally, like homework, worksheets should be written so they can prepare students for a topic, endorse something they are currently learning, or as a revision exercise. They should supplement and build on skills, themes and ideas, but they can also introduce something different to give students a brief taste or understanding of another aspect of the subject that you are not covering in 'normal' lessons.

Cover work

Setting cover work, especially in a practical subject like art, can often be a nuisance and is usually unplanned and needs to be fairly instant. When you're in the middle of a practical part of a project and you're off sick, going on a school trip or invigilating a GCSE or A level art exam, it's not always feasible to let students continue without you and cover teachers cannot be expected to supervise complicated or specialist equipment or activities.

Time spent writing worksheets that will augment students'

studies without requiring them to work with technical or specialized materials that require your input or guidance will actually reduce your workload in the long run, and colleagues will be grateful to you for writing them! They can be useful in helping students integrate class work with homework or to help them to focus on particular aspects you want them to understand in more detail. The worksheets in this book and online are only suggestions and will probably need adaptation to suit different departmental needs. Some worksheet examples can be found below.

YEAR 7 – SIGNS OF THE ZODIAC

This worksheet can be used for a one-off lesson or can be extended to take a longer period of time. It also works well as a homework task. Pupils could be put into groups and told to select one zodiac sign each, all working together to produce the twelve signs.

'Zodiac' is Greek for 'circle of animals.' There are twelve zodiac signs, each representing approximately one month in the year. Many illustrators and artists have designed zodiac signs and now it's your turn. The twelve zodiac signs are:

Aquarius (the water carrier) 20th January–18th February *(air)*
Pisces (the fish) 19th February–20th March *(water)*
Aries (the ram) 21st March–19th April *(fire)*
Taurus (the bull) 20th April–20th May *(earth)*
Gemini (the twins) 21st May–21st June *(air)*
Cancer (the crab) 22nd June–22nd July *(water)*
Leo (the lion) 23rd July–22nd August *(fire)*
Virgo (the virgin) 23rd August–22nd September *(earth)*
Libra (the scales) 23rd September–23rd October *(air)*
Scorpio (the scorpion) 24th October–21st November *(water)*
Sagittarius (the archer) 22nd November–21st December *(fire)*
Capricorn (the goat) 22nd December–19th January *(earth)*

Research ideas from books, magazines and the internet then make visual and written notes, planning and forming ideas for your own design for one zodiac sign. Next, try out several different ideas for your design and choose one idea for your final image. Complete this using a variety of sources – primary and secondary. Fill an A4 page with your final, coloured and detailed design.

YEAR 7 – ILLUMINATED MANUSCRIPTS

This worksheet can be used as an extension to an ongoing illuminated letter project or any project concerned with Celtic design, medieval art, book illustration or calligraphy. It can be used as a follow-up to a visit to a relevant site or museum, as an extension sheet or as an extended homework project.

Aims/objectives: You are going to demonstrate your knowledge and understanding of medieval manuscript writing and lettering, to create a completed illuminated page design of your own. At the end of this piece of work, you will understand how to apply certain types of paint and other dry media to create the appearance of an ancient manuscript. You will also be aware of the reasons illuminated manuscripts were produced and how they were made and will be able to make connections between your own work and the work of ancient artists. In creating your own modern illuminated page, you will use your knowledge and understanding, to modify and improve your work.

Key vocabulary: illumination, manuscript, scribes, gilding, gold leaf, thumbnail sketches

Time: Approximately three lessons

Materials: Information and images of medieval illuminated manuscripts; cartridge paper, pencils, paints and coloured pencils.

Your task: Study a book of hours – online, in books and/or at a museum. Research why monks produced illuminated manuscripts and what materials they used. Look at various styles of lettering. Compare medieval illuminated manuscripts to your homework, school or daily planner. Select a significant day in the year such as Easter, Diwali, Eid-Ul-Adha, Succoth, school sports day, school production, your birthday or the first day of summer and plan and create a page for your planner, using illuminations that correspond to your chosen modern celebration. Use elements of design that medieval artists used to construct their illuminated manuscripts.

Tips: Begin with thumbnail sketches to develop your ideas. Then plan your illuminated page, drawing lightly with a 2B pencil. Use your research to 'borrow' and adapt shapes, objects and colours for your final design. Once you are happy with your design. Check the aims/objectives from time-to-time to check that you are meeting the objectives.

Evaluation: Check the aims/objectives. Do you feel you met them all? If you have, do you think you worked as hard as you could and have produced the best piece of work in the time that you could manage? If not, what could you have improved?

YEAR 8 – AFRICAN ART

This worksheet should include images to inspire pupils and could be used either in class or as a homework activity. It could be extended to incorporate a wider range of art from other cultures and could constitute an ongoing year-long homework project that results in a booklet full of research and practical activities showing an understanding of the art and crafts of other cultures.

In most African languages there is no word for 'art' and its function is far more important than its quality. African art is not made to look beautiful, but usually to help people connect to the spirit world, to serve a religious purpose, to celebrate (for example a birth or a good harvest) or to commemorate an important event. Spirits in Africa include the dead (or ancestors) and the spirits of rivers, lakes, plants, trees, mountains, weather and the sun and moon. African artists produce images of their god or gods or of the spirits or other objects, such as Ashanti doll figures – dolls that are given to girls when they come of age, which they keep until they have a child. Many African art objects are based on human figures and features, including masks and many different African cultures use them in different ways.

Your task is to design a mask, based on research of African art. Create a mask featuring patterns, shapes and colours that include decorations and shapes that are characteristic of African masks you have researched. You may use collage materials to embellish your final design.

YEAR 9 – SYNAESTHESIA

This worksheet will enhance many ongoing units you may be teaching during Key Stage 3 or it can be used as a standalone, interesting topic that is useful for students to understand and think about even if they are not covering the area in schemes of work.

Wassily Kandinsky had Synaesthesia. This meant that when he heard music, he 'saw' colours and shapes in his mind. People with Synaesthesia often perceive words, numbers and letters as colours and shapes in their minds. Kandinsky wrote about colour and spiritual, mystical theories. He began painting abstract images and called them harmonies or compositions because he said that music did not have to be named after 'things' in the real world, but was appreciated for itself alone. He said: 'Colour is the keyboard, the eyes are the harmonies, the soul is the piano with many strings. The artist is the hand that plays, touching one key then another to cause vibration in the soul.'

Your task:
Imagine a song or piece of music in your head. 'Listen' to it silently and make doodles in your sketchbook, describing it visually. You may wish to use colour and/or to show textures and you may wish to work across a large sheet of paper or two pages in your sketchbook as you work out your ideas. Consider what elements will show rhythm or harmony in your image? How will you show higher or lower notes? What will you do to represent loud or quieter sounds and how will you make the 'mood' of the music apparent to anyone looking at your work?

YEAR 9 WORKSHEET: PORTRAITS

This worksheet is useful for a teacher absent lesson, as an extension to the illuminated letter project, as a follow-up to a visit to a relevant site or museum, as an extension sheet or as an extended homework project.

Aims/objectives: You are going to look at portraits and understand the ways in which artists have produced images of their friends, family and people around them, using a variety of techniques. By analysing particular artist's use of media and technique, you will learn how they produced certain portraits and how you can adapt and use these methods for your own portrait.

Key Vocabulary: portrait, hatching, cross-hatching, stippling, impasto, facial proportions, characteristics, features

Time: Approximately three lessons

Materials: copies of portraits by other artists, such as Rembrandt, van Gogh, Sargent, Holbein; cartridge paper, pencils, paints, coloured pencils and fine liners or dip pens and ink.

Your task: Look closely at a portrait painted by one of the artists your teacher has provided. How many types of line or brush marks can you see? In your sketchbook, describe the different brush marks or lines you can see in the portrait. Describe the expression on the sitter's face. How does the facial expression compare with the type of line or brush marks? Do they complement or contrast with each other? What do you think the person is/ was like? Do you think the artist has captured a lifelike portrait? How has he or she made it look realistic? If it is not realistic, how and why has the artist distorted reality? How has the artist created contrast and shade in his or her technique? Can you read any message(s) in this portrait? Now you are going to create a portrait of a friend using similar techniques as those used by the artist you are studying. First of all, choose a friend! Double-check his or her facial proportions, such as distances and shapes between features. Mark these on carefully and then use the technique of your chosen artist, such as hatching and crosshatching or impasto paint to create the look of three dimensions. Using whatever material you decide suits your style of portrait, keep practising the techniques your artist used.

Assessment: You will be assessed on your understanding of facial proportions and characteristics, and the technique reflecting your chosen artist used in your portrait. Although your portrait style reflects your understanding of your chosen artist, it should also reflect your own personal choices (of materials, style and expression) and your developing technical skill.

YEAR 10 – TREES AND FORESTS

This can be used either in class for several lessons, perhaps as an introductory mini-project when they first start their GCSE course or as an ongoing homework resource.

1. Using resources such as books from the art room collection or school library and/or the internet, investigate trees and anything relating to them, such as branches, leaves, berries and buds etc. Find an image by an artist or designer of trees or parts of trees and copy it, using only hatched lines – no outlines. Build up details with hatched lines in a variety of directions and length and cross-hatching to show depth and/or texture.

2. Find a tree and draw four detailed sections, showing tone and texture. Colour is optional

3. Select one of the sections you drew from direct observation and draw a more in-depth section of that. Show detail clearly – use pen and ink or pencil for this.

4. Study the work of William Morris (such as Acanthus, Willow Bough, Jasmine or the Woodpecker); or the work of John Henry Dearle or Charles Francis Annesley Voysey. Design your own wallpaper panel based on your own drawings and the Arts and Crafts designs you have been investigating.

5. Write about the work of the designer you have looked at and evaluate his and your own work. What appeals to you about the work; what did you try to do with your own response; what materials have you used; what materials did the designer use; what colours are most effective and why; how could you improve a) the work of your chosen designer and b) your own work?

6. Design a) a print (you may use lino, batik or screen) and b) a ceramic tile in relief based on the work you have been doing.

7. Go out and sketch several trees looking at different
   (a) angles   (b) amounts of detail
   (c) dimensions   (d) materials

8. Compile some pages in your sketchbook that builds up your knowledge of trees. Include notes and sketches about different trees; collect leaves, bits of bark and so on and stick these in your sketchbook; make bark rubbings and add annotations. Make thumbnail sketches about different shapes of trees and their leaves; try out paint and other materials to replicate colours, blends of colours and textures and make notes, such as: how is it shaped; how tall is it; do the branches point upwards or downwards and are the leaves large, small, dense or sparse?

9. Create a pattern from your observations – this can be regular or irregular.

10. Finally, create a mixed media painting of trees. This can be a menacing forest (look at the work of De Chirico – how did he make an image look threatening)? It could be a natural landscape (consider the work of Constable). Or it could be in a naïve style (Rousseau created images of jungles without ever having seen one). Whatever you decide to do, find an artist to respond to who has either done something similar or whose style you admire and feel would work well if incorporated into the style or process you will be using.

KS3 Theory & Practical Worksheet: Turner & Light

This works well for any lessons when the art teacher is absent for whatever reason; as a follow-up to a visit to a gallery or a lesson on any related subjects; as an extension activity or to be used when the class is not in the art rooms.

Introduction: Joseph Mallord William Turner (1775–1851) introduced a new and revolutionary approach to landscape. Rather than simply represent objects he saw, he focused more on the quality of light and atmosphere in his subjects. Throughout his life, he was fascinated by the sun and the effects of light. He continued to paint conventional pictures, but many of his paintings became increasingly dramatic and with a strong sense of movement. Throughout his life he kept a sketchbook of scenes he later developed in his studio into large paintings. By the 1830s, his brushwork had become freer and his colours seemed to dissolve into each other. John Constable (1775–1837) said of his work: 'He seems to paint with tinted steam, so evanescent and so airy.'

Consider: Turner's style may seem familiar to us now, but his paintings were remarkable for their time and many people violently criticised them. His brushstrokes and exaggerated colour combinations confidently created a feeling of depth, space' light and atmosphere. How do you show the effects of light in your paintings? What colours do you use to show brightness? What colours do you use to show depth? Do colours look the same in the early morning light and in the late afternoon light? In your sketchbook, divide a page into five columns and 1) list the colours you might use in a painting of the dawn. 2) Next to this, list the colours you might use in a painting of the sunset. 3) Do the same for a painting of the dusk; 4) for a painting of the night and 5) for a painting of the middle of the day. Find any work by Turner. Look at the way in which he paints shadows and light. Notice how he paints with atmospheric perspective – making distant forms fainter and bluer and nearer objects warmer and more contrasting. Notice that his application of paint is usually thin and clear, yet expressive.

Your task:

1. Using watercolours and watercolour paper or thick paper that you have stretched, paint an imaginary landscape, letting the paint flow

as Turner did. Be aware where the light is coming from and where the shadows fall.

2. Using sunlight effects as a starting point, you should produce a collage of any landscape of your choice. You should gather some reference material and use a variety of materials to build up your landscape. Again, consider where the light falls – and where it doesn't!

KS3 PRACTICAL WORKSHEET (1)

This worksheet is useful for occasions when teachers are absent or you are not in the art rooms. It is probably more suitable for older students rather than younger.

Constructing the human head with line and shading
Many artists have had different ideas about constructing faces with lines and then adding tones to them. These include Juan Gris (1887–1927), Albert Gleizes (1881–1953), Jean Metzinger (1883–1956) and Naum Gabo (1890–1977).

Your task: Construct a human face with geometric lines and then add tones with graphite pencils or coloured pencils. Explore several ideas in your sketchbook and then draw a large, final picture that uses the techniques you consider to be the most effective.

KS3 PRACTICAL WORKSHEET (2)

This is a three-lesson worksheet, which could come in handy if you are absent for more than one lesson (it takes about three lessons). In addition to the worksheet, provide students with a number of images of dancers.

Figure movement
1. In your sketchbook, use some of the dance pictures provided to create three compositions showing movement. Don't try to copy the images exactly, but concentrate on proportion, tone and movement to create your own interpretation of dancers.
   Homework: Collect several pictures showing moving figures. Draw and colour one of these.
2. Use your own pictures as a reference. In your sketchbook once again produce three compositions showing movement and dance. Consider elements of composition, including a main centre of interest or focal point, overlapping shapes, negative space, lines, balance, proportion and tonal contrasts.
   Homework: Research the artist Edgar Degas (1834–1917). Study his compositions: how did he arrange his paintings? Write a paragraph and draw two outline pictures to illustrate this.
3. Complete a final piece on A2 paper. Lightly and carefully map out your ideas. Remember to show that you have considered

composition. Look at: the shapes in between, the figures, the proportion of the figures, the tone (light and shade). Ask yourself 'how interesting is my composition?' Colour your work using paint, oil pastels or felt tipped pens.

Homework: Evaluate your work – what have you learned?

GCSE, AS and A2 $\boxed{12}$

GCSE and A level art and design courses are intended to extend and build on students' learning in the subject at KS3. A level art and design incorporates an even wider and more intense programme of study. In addition, an increasing number of post-16 art and design qualifications have been introduced in recent years to provide closer links with vocational areas. Many of the newer qualifications have similar content and structure to art and design GCSEs and A levels, but have been introduced to meet more specialized needs. While they are more suitable for some students, GCSE and A level remain the broad based, academic routes. Although the vocational qualifications are not discussed fully here, many of the areas covered in this book can be transferred or adapted for them.

The structure of GCSE and A level art and design courses

Among other things, art and design at GCSE and A level should develop students' skills in analysis and experimentation as well as practical, technical and expressive skills, their aesthetic understanding, critical judgement, creative thinking and independence of mind. GCSE is usually completed over two years and comprises coursework and a controlled or timed test (also known as the 'set task unit'). Progressing from that, A level usually takes two years and comprises the AS coursework and timed test and the A2 coursework and timed test, which together make up a complete A level. AS can be taken as a qualification in its own right or can be continued as the first half of a full A level. Both GCSE and A level are assessed synoptically.

Your department may be following the endorsed or unendorsed GCSE or A level courses and you may be offering a

151

short GCSE course alongside the full GCSE course. Art departments and schools usually choose which qualifications to offer and which exam board to use as suits their methods of teaching and school structure. GCSE art and design courses consist of between two and four units of coursework, including a final exam, depending on which board you use. Short GCSE courses consist of between two and three units plus an exam. AS and A2 both consist of two or three units each: one or two of coursework and one exam. The AS makes up exactly 50 per cent of the entire A level mark.

◆ GCSE controlled assessments

Some exam boards now call GCSE coursework 'controlled assessments'. Brought in by QCA in order to reduce the risk of plagiarism, this means that all work must be produced under controlled conditions. The key matter in controlled assessment is the question of authentication. All coursework (called a portfolio of work by the exam boards) has to be completed in a set amount of time (usually 45 hours). Teachers must authenticate all work submitted as the candidate's own work. This does not mean that a candidate must be supervised throughout the completion of all work but the teacher must exercise sufficient supervision, or introduce sufficient checks, to be in a position to authenticate the work. Therefore photographs, image-making studies, colour studies, experiments with media and so on arising from homework and so undertaken independently without direct supervision must be assessed by the teacher and determined to be the student's own work. Provided the teacher feels confident that students' work is their own, this work can be submitted. You should therefore be as familiar as possible with your own students' styles, approaches, interests and methods.

◆ Externally set assignments

At or near the end of their course, GCSE students take a ten hour controlled test, which comes after four to eight weeks of preparation and is worth about 40 per cent of the total GCSE marks. This should be completed over two or more days and should be a 'sustained, focused study'. The AS controlled test or externally set assignment, which is taken at or near the end of the course, is between five and eight hours and is worth between 40 and 50 per cent of the AS or 20–25 per cent of the complete A level. The AS exam is shorter than the GCSE because when in

2000 the A level was altered to incorporate AS and A2, the full A level exam of 20 hours was divided. All exam boards agreed that the A2 externally set assignment should be longer than AS, so each board chose their own exam lengths. The AS exam, being shorter than the GCSE, gives students another challenge: they should be able to produce better quality and more in depth work than they managed in the ten hour GCSE exam. The A2 externally set assignment, which is either 12 or 15 hours in length, should also show progression. As far as requirements go, all the exam boards adhere to the same principles but they vary in their approaches. Mark schemes too, although similar, differ slightly between boards, although overall expectations correspond and QCA oversees them to ensure uniformity. Your department might run the endorsed or unendorsed options. The unendorsed options are broad based, where students can work in several areas of study. Endorsed options are specialized courses that include:

- fine art (which can include drawing, painting, sculpture, land art, installation, printmaking, film, video, mixed media or new media)
- 3D design (which can include ceramics, sculpture, theatre, television, film and/or exhibition design, jewellery, interior, product, environmental design or architecture)
- textiles (which can include printed and/or dyed materials, domestic textiles, constructed textiles, applied textiles, fashion, costume)
- graphic communication (which can include computer-aided design, illustration, advertising, packaging, digital imaging, film, video or animation)
- photography (which can include portraiture, documentary, still life, photo-journalism, environmental photography, experimental imagery, photographic installation, video and film) or
- critical and contextual studies (including investigation and study across art, craft and design).

◆ New media

Students are allowed to work with new media within any endorsement as long as they meet the aims and assessment objectives of the qualification. This is the crux of the matter. Many students, particularly boys, are attracted to digital or computerized work, which is encouraging, but you must make sure that they meet all the assessment objectives. It might mean a sketchbook full of drawings, paint experiments and analysis or you might find they can address the criteria solely using new media. Just make sure they are aware of this as some fantastic work is being produced in this area.

Students just have to understand that the objectives are necessary in order to keep the qualifications fair and impartial. They should use appropriate equipment and software to explore and experiment with computer-generated artwork, including drawings, animation (which can be in virtual 2D or 3D) or stop frame or stop motion work. If they choose to take this route for the whole or part of their work, they must still show evidence of the design process and of the alternative solutions that have been considered, through rough visuals and storyboards. The use of sound should also be considered and students should be able to produce, use and/or explain chosen tracks or sounds they have incorporated.

◆ Units and assessment

Assessment objectives, as discussed in Chapters 3, 7 and 9, should be understood by every student. As soon as they begin the GCSE and A level courses, give everyone a simplified copy (such as the versions in Chapters 3 and 9) and discuss them so often that everything becomes second nature. Keep emphasizing the importance of covering every objective in their coursework and exam or they will lose marks. Depending on which board your school is following, the amount of preparation time students are allowed before the final exam varies. This table shows the number of coursework units required by each exam board:

Exam boards	Number of units required by each board
AQA	2, 3, 4 units
EDEXCEL	2 units
OCR	3 units
WJEC/CBAC	2 units
CCEA	2 units

Here are the different preparation periods and supervised times given by different boards:

Exam boards	Preparation period	Exam time
AQA	4 weeks	10 hours
EDEXCEL	8 weeks	10 hours
OCR	6 weeks	10 hours
WJEC/CBAC	6 weeks	10 hours
CCEA	10 weeks	10 hours

AS and A2 externally set assignments also vary, but in total the two A level exams equal 20 hours. You will receive the paper before February and you are allowed to give it to students from 1 February each year. Papers for GCSE and A level are usually A4 booklets, generally consisting of one or two broad based thematic starting points. The latest papers include both text based and visual starting points. Students are given a particular time period, as a rule between four and six weeks, to prepare for the exam, which must be completed and moderated internally by mid-May. This table shows the preparation and exam time lengths for each examination board:

Exam boards	Prep time and AS exam	Prep time and A2 exam
AQA	(4 weeks prep) 5 hours	(4 weeks prep) 10 hours
EDEXCEL	(school's choice) 8 hours	(school's choice) 12 hours
OCR	(3–6 weeks prep) 5 hours	(3–6 weeks prep) 15 hours
WJEC/CBAC	(school's choice) 8 hours	(school's choice) 12 hours
CCEA	(school's choice) 8 hours	(school's choice) 12 hours

Guiding students

Both coursework and preparatory studies should be continuous periods of focused study. So when they have received their exam papers, students should either have finished all coursework or put it aside until the exam is over. They should concentrate on the exam preparation until it is over. This is important so they fulfil all the assessment objectives thoroughly and do not miss out anything vital. To cover all requirements, they must produce a variety of work including mind mapping, researching and experimenting with techniques, materials and ideas, analyzing and investigating and looking in detail at their ideas and the ways in which similar topics have been broached by others. Most of this work will be recorded in their work journals but some, such as 3D work, printing or large paintings, will necessarily be produced outside the journal.

Make sure that everyone understands the difference between primary and secondary sources. Emphasize the importance of originality and make sure they know that everything must be their own work. If they copy someone else's work, they must explain what they have learnt from this and show how they can develop ideas and responses from other people's work to produce something original. They must ensure that all work is annotated clearly and thoroughly, while sources, evidence and data should

Expressive AS coursework – A1 work journal and painting. Westcliff High School for Girls, Westcliff-on-Sea, Essex

also be listed. Let them know that a momentary thought or idea is best jotted down in the work journal as soon, or almost as soon, as it occurs. Tell them never to discard anything they produce, as even unsuccessful or incomplete work can demonstrate effort, experimentation and risk taking to examiners and often display other attributes that have the potential to gain marks.

Students often ask how much work is enough, but that is an unanswerable question so it is a good idea to give them a general checklist to make sure that they work in the right way for each unit, including their exam preparation:

- List ideas about the theme you have been given and develop your ideas from personal interests and experiences.
- Work out a mind map to generate more ideas.
- Bounce ideas off friends, family and your art teacher.
- Select three or four of your favourite ideas. Select two or three of these promising 'routes'. How would you develop these? Do any reach dead ends? Do any seem to lead on to further possibilities?
- Draw objects and ideas from primary and secondary sources; take related photos and write notes.
- Continue jotting down ideas, trying out materials and techniques until one of your routes (initial ideas) becomes more obviously the area that interests you. Follow that idea in more depth.
- How have other artists, craftspeople or designers responded to similar themes? Look at how your idea has been approached by different cultures. Collect images by these artists as well as any other images that link to your theme from magazines, the internet, photocopies from books, leaflets and so on. Make drawings and studies from their work to try to understand how and why they have used materials and techniques. Comment about the artists' and your own work.
- Experiment with ideas for paintings, sculptures, prints, films, photography, collage and anything else you can think of on your theme; show that you have tried out different materials and techniques.
- Then decide what works and what needs modifying or discarding.
- Develop ideas for your final piece of work based on the theme, showing that you have responded to the work of other artists. Show how your ideas have developed from the start of your project to the end. Include an evaluation of your work.

This checklist will work for both GCSE and A level, although A level necessarily requires deeper research, a larger number of and

GCSE sketchbook explorations. Westcliff High School for Girls, Westcliff-on-Sea, Essex

better quality drawings and experimentation and even more risk taking. Drawing skills need to be fluent, but remind pupils that drawing is not just about making marks on white paper with pencils. In your efforts to make your students more imaginative, suggest ideas such as drawing with: needles and thread on fabric; cocktail sticks on a thick base of paint; chalks or pastels on damp watercolour paper; pen and wash; pen and ink; sand on card; silverpoint; pencil or charcoal shavings spread with a *torchon*; or computer-generated drawings.

It is important that students explore their ideas through analyzing the work of others. You can help them do this by emphasizing the need to consider the artist or designer's intentions. They can only do this well when they understand the artist's context, i.e. where and when he or she was born, the work's remit and the cultural, social and political background of when the work was made. Biographical details should only be included if they are relevant to the student's work. Once you have clarified this way of researching, let students work independently so they can choose their own sources and uncover their own details and ideas.

At the start of the GCSE course (and they may need reminding at the start of the AS course too), provide a structured research method to help them in their hunt for relevant information. You could provide a list of questions or headings that they always consider for any artist or artwork, such as those in Chapter 10 and online. It is important that students compare the work of artists across different time periods and cultures, so developing an understanding of why some works were produced, why they looked as they did, why certain materials were used and why they were groundbreaking or particularly significant. There is no need for them to write entire essays explaining all they understand about an artist or a piece of work, but they should be fairly discriminatory, focusing only on what is pertinent to their own work and investigations. Tell them not to include irrelevant or meaningless source material in their research and writing, but remind them of the need to evaluate as they work as this is far easier than returning to it after they have finished. Photocopying from books or copying and pasting from the internet will nearly always be irrelevant.

Too much writing can detract from the artwork, so make sure that just as they decide what to change in their practical work, they should be discriminating and selective over what they write. They should only write where words will explain the artwork in a way that the art cannot. Writing should not repeat what they have shown visually, but should add something further to the understanding. There is a sample self-assessment sheet online that you could give to all exam students. Although it is not suitable for all students, if they use it, it will help them to consider each unit as a whole.

Exam necessities

Each board sets the exam titles for GCSE, AS and A2, which are taken by all entrants during the summer term. The topics are new every year and are words or phrases that allow for open interpretation, such as 'knots', 'change', 'sanctuary', 'discord', 'growth', 'colour', 'time', 'structures', 'shadows and silhouettes' or 'celebration'. All the exam boards suggest starting points for their themes, including ideas, websites and names of pertinent artists, craftspeople and designers. You will also need to help them to begin coming up with ideas and solving creative problems. Art teachers do this in a variety of ways, including:

Flowers inspired by Georgia O'Keeffe. Westcliff High School for Girls, Westcliff-on-Sea, Essex

Bold brush marks and tonal contrasts describe objects, facial expression and a reflection. Westcliff High School for Girls, Westcliff-on-Sea, Essex

creating and showing students a PowerPoint of starting points and artists who have responded to similar themes; a huge wall display where you and colleagues stick up a medley of images to inspire students; or a booklet that takes them through various areas they could consider and steps they should take to fulfil all assessment objectives. There is no set method for initiating the creative problem-solving process, but several have already been discussed in this book, for instance in Chapters 1, 2, 5, 7, 8 and 9, and additional material is available online.

Explain to students that the theme is their creative problem. When they receive their paper, they should imagine their theme is in a box. It is their job to open the box and create something original and meaningful. Always show students how their investigations of the title can be as broad and as limitless as they can manage, as long as they show moderators their thought processes and how they reached their final ideas through preparatory studies. Advise them to produce as much work before the exam as they can and to work out – without having a run-through of the exact piece – what they will do in their exam.

All preparatory work must be handed in at the end of the exam but coursework may resume if there is time before students take their other exams and the moderator has visited (this usually takes place in June). During the exam, you are not allowed to discuss the 'artistic' quality of a student's work, but you can give technical assistance where needed. Some things can be prepared by students before the exam, such as the stretching of a canvas, arrangement of a still life, preparation of a block for printing, or drying and firing time for sculptural work. You cannot allow students to undertake any preparation that constitutes part of the work, such as preparing clay or drawing a preparatory outline for a painting. Everyone needs to be aware of the differences between preparing for their final exam pieces, which is permitted, and starting the work, which is not.

◆ Taking care of students' work

It is necessary to keep all work safely, but particularly at GCSE and A level. Several methods work well, although you must emphasize from the start of the course that all students must take responsibility for their own work and not leave anything lying around in between lessons. Methods of safe keeping include: asking all students to buy their own A1 folder at the start of their course; having a large plan chest in which students keep their work in their own, labelled drawers; or cupboards or shelves within cupboards, also clearly marked for specific year groups or forms. Three-dimensional work should be stored on high shelves, on top of a sturdy cupboard or in a store cupboard. Important work should be photographed while in progress and once it is completed, just in case it is broken or mislaid. All work should be labelled clearly with the student's name, form and level. When work is being entered for GCSE, AS or A2, all work must be marked with:

- school or college name and centre number
- the individual's name and candidate number
- the specification title and code
- the assignment title and unit number.

To clarify things for moderating, it's worth having labels in one colour for coursework; another for exam preparatory studies; and a third for the exam final piece. You can either get students to colour labels with thick felt tips or ask your reprographics department to print sticky labels in three different colours. You are allowed to help students present their GCSE and A level submissions and schools usually have their own methods of doing this. Some have full-scale exhibitions that remain up for parents and friends to visit after moderation has finished; others submit portfolios; others still have selected work on display, such as the final pieces, with coursework and preparatory studies kept neatly to one side.

◆ *Preparing for the exam*

There is no set number of words that students must write in their coursework or preliminary studies, but they must include some information about their thought processes, ideas and methods. They should annotate their research and visual explorations in order to prove to the moderator that they have covered all the necessary factors to meet the assessment objectives. Explain to students that their work journals or sketchbooks are their dialogues with the moderator as they will not be there to explain it when he or she is looking at their work. Work journals, as discussed in Chapter 7, do not have to be books, nor do students have to have new work journals for each unit, but this would be more straightforward for moderation purposes. Units must be kept separate in some way from each other.

When considering the work of others, students can investigate both famous and little-known artists or designers. The exam boards ask them to make 'informed connections', which means that they should explain how they see links between their own and other artists' work. Whatever art students find to study, encourage them to go and see the work at firsthand if they can. Sometimes, lesser-known artists are willing to respond to letters, emails or questionnaires, which can be exceptionally helpful.

Before the controlled test, every student should discuss in detail with you what they intend to do. You will be able to advise them whether they are being over ambitious, too tame, or whether there are any other factors they should consider. You might need to show them a technique or suggest an artist, but as a rule they should not try out new materials or methods during an exam.

During the exam, students should fill the time producing one or more pieces that they have fully planned and explained in their preliminary work. Because the exams are spread over two or three days, they should have an idea of how much they should have done by a certain time and discipline themselves and their time accordingly. As a general rule, smaller work should be more detailed and larger work can be less so. For the preparatory work quality and relevance matters more than quantity, although there needs to be a substantial amount of work in order to meet the assessment objectives sufficiently. The final piece produced during the exam should be thorough, thoughtful and appropriate and should be a realization of all the work produced during the planning and preliminary period. It should be as varied as your students, that is: executed extremely well, an amazing idea the culmination of a thorough and unexpected investigation, or all of these and more. Their final task is to write an evaluation of what they did, why they did it and how it worked out.

◆ The personal investigation or study

By the time a student takes A2 art and design, they should be demonstrating more maturity in their work, greater technical abilities and understanding of their own interests in connection with the wider world. The coursework undertaken at A2 has to be produced alongside a related personal study of between 1,000 and 3,000 words. (This works out between three and ten typed pages of A4 in 12 point.) This investigation must be based on an idea, issue, concept or theme leading to a finished piece or pieces and should evolve from each student's practical coursework. Each personal study should be about a topic that interests the student, should be linked with some aspect of contemporary or past artists, designers or craftspeople and clearly connects with their practical work. As many students find making connections between their practical work and their own interests difficult, you might have to help them to decide. Sometimes a connection is obvious, but often it is more obscure, so you might need to help them to find something relevant. This could be looking at colour in landscape art; studying the work of particular Spanish artists; comparing techniques of painting skin tones and textures; perspective techniques in painting; how sculptors have created a sense of solidity; or how certain architects have responded to the natural world. A personal study outline can be found online and below.

Like coursework, the personal study is internally set, assessed by teachers and externally moderated. It will always be related to the endorsement that individuals are taking and must always be relevant to the practical work the student is undertaking for A2 coursework. It can take the form of a written, critical, analytical study; a journal; a log; a video; or something similar. Students need to submit a proposal or outline of their proposed personal study to you so you can check on their planning and intentions. In this, they should explain what they are hoping to find out and what firsthand sources they will be looking at. (This does not necessarily mean that they have to visit galleries, there is a great deal of art and design all around us; encourage them to be imaginative.) This is where key vocabulary should be used and sources should be identified and acknowledged. Here is a checklist to help your students get started:

- Think about artists or art movements whose work you feel strongly about and can be seen to link in some way with the practical work you are doing.
- If you pose a question, you will find it easier to write a response. Questions could encompass: comparing the work of artists; how particular artists have used colour, texture or light; what or who has influenced certain artists; how women and men have represented women; or how have certain designers used nature as a basis for their work?
- The study must be your personal response to the art. It must be written from your perspective and include your opinions and feelings. Why do you think this? What connections can you make

between the artist's work and your own? What feelings does an artist evoke in you and why?

- Notes on style: a) you need to integrate images with the writing – always remember that this is art and design so your artwork matters; b) *how* you write something is as important as *what* you write, so use key vocabulary and intelligent research. Never use foul language or you will seem as though you have a poor vocabulary.
- Artists' biographical details should be brief. You should always include a contents page, introduction and conclusion. Add a bibliography and list any resources you used, such as books, museums, galleries or websites.
- Most important of all perhaps is the importance of viewing some of the work at first hand (primary sources). Try to go and see some of the work and make sure that you show how you did in your study.

Personal Study initial outline plan

Title (you can write this later):

_____

Aims (write a short paragraph about what you are interested in):

_____

_____

_____

_____

_____

Chapter plan (this should include an introduction and a conclusion, but it does not have to follow this pattern – i.e. you can have more or less chapters):

1. Introduction (_____words) State briefly what you have chosen to study, why you have chosen it and some of the artists/works you will be looking at:

   _____

   _____

2. (_____words) Content:

   _____

   _____

3. (_____words) Content:

   _____

   _____

4. (_____words) Content:

   _____

   _____

5. Conclusion (_____words) What I have learned and how I will use it in my Practical Personal Investigation:

   _____

   _____

Primary sources (things you have seen at first hand – galleries, an artist at work etc):

Bibliography and Secondary sources (including books, magazines, websites, exhibition catalogues etc):

(You must also include a contents page)

Assessment objectives

AO1 = Visual recording – make sure you create lots of relevant images, such as: drawings, paintings, responses to sections of paintings (e.g. in different materials/ same idea, different subject/ different colours/ different scale etc) and make the whole thing look good

AO2 = Critical thinking – you must analyse; it's not enough to say you like a work. You should say instead that it's successful because, or compare it to something else. There are some suggestions following this about questions to ask yourself when looking at art.

AO3 = Practical research – they want you to 'develop ideas through sustained investigations', which means lots of different ideas in your art work – try to think of different ways to show you have really looked into your topic and kept enquiring.

AO4 = Personal development – it has to be personal to you – it can't be taken from something you've seen in another book or on a website. Write and produce images that are personal to the interest you've shown in your study.

Questions to ask yourself when looking at art

Subject
Key questions:
Content – What is the work about? What is happening?
Message – What question is the work asking? Is it asking us to respond in a particular way? Is it a story, a riddle, a command or a challenge for instance? Can you recognise any symbols?
Title – What is it called? Does this change your opinion of the work?

Object
Key questions:
Colour/shape/marks/surface/composition – What are the 'formal aspects' of the work?
Materials – What is the work made of? Traditional materials or unexpected? Is the material important to the work?
Process – How has the work been made? What skills were involved? How visible or invisible is the process of making? How did the artist produce it?
Scale – How big is the work? Why is it this size? Would its meaning change if it was a different size?
Space/position/environment – Is there an illusion of space in the work or has the artist rejected illusion and emphasised flatness? How does the work relate to space around it?
Time – Does the work demand a certain amount of your time or does it change for you over time? Do you have any particular connections with the work from personal experience?

Context
Key questions:
When/where – When and where was the work made? Does this give another 'dimension' to it? What 'history' does it represent?
Who – Who made it and who was it made for?
Now – How do people view the work today? Is it different from the way it might have been seen when it was made? How and why has opinion changed?

Personal
Key questions:
Myself – What are my first reactions to the work? Why does it make me think or feel this way? How does who I am (where I live, my family, my beliefs and friends etc) affect the way I view the work? How do my responses reveal my attitudes and values? How do my opinions change when discussing the work with others?
My world – What does the work remind me of? Why does it remind me of that? How does my background affect my reactions? How are my responses similar or different from those around me?
My experience – We all bring different experiences and interests to looking at art. This could come from a part time job, your family, places you have visited, things you have seen on TV etc. How does your reaction differ from your friends' reactions?

As they did for each of the other units at GCSE and AS, students must use a work journal for their personal studies. In this case, the work journal must be used for gathering research, collecting and documenting evidence that they have been considering the work of others and their own responses to relevant artists. The final piece will be the actual personal study, which must be presented well. It can be a book, a relevant piece of artwork with accompanying notes, a video or audio recording, again with accompanying transcripts or anything else that the student deems is appropriate for his or her personal study.

Further resources

A list of web-based resources to accompany this book is available online. Web resources include: education authorities, unions, exam boards, useful museum and gallery websites and some useful art reference sites. There is also a list of qualifications in England, Scotland and Wales.

Index